& PREPARE

PURPOSE

IVE

RESILIENT IVF BU

URVIVE & GROW LEA

BUILD REDEFINE SUCCESS

AWARE

OVERCOME CHALLENGE

RESILIENT

LEADERSHIP

BE RESOURCEFUL

VATE

STRATEGY

MONITOR PROGRESS ADAP

CREATE VALUE

COORDINATE

EXECUTE BRILLIANTLY

BE CREATIVE

CREATIVE

PROVISE MOTIVATE ADAPT

THE RIGHT PEOPLE CELEBRATE

BEYOND
STRATEGY

LEADING YOUR ORGANIZATION
TO REMARKABLE GROWTH

MICHAEL KOULY

First Edition

ISBN 978-0-9992181-7-4

*To all those who are striving to
make their organizations, countries,
and the world a better place*

CONTENTS

PREFACE

Writing this book took four years of intense empirical research, which topped some 30 years of practical immersion in the fields of strategy and leadership. The book is also the result of scholarly work with pioneers in strategy and leadership at the Harvard Business School and the Harvard Kennedy School of Government.

The intention of the book is to explore a theory that I have called the Purpose-Driven Growth Model (PDG). I developed the PDG Model after spending years observing (as a CEO, an advisor to boards of directors, and a teacher of executive education) organizations lose opportunities, remain stagnant, and sometimes fail because of strategy and leadership issues.

I saw even the smartest strategies, designed by famous global consulting firms, collapse due to lack of essential leadership. I also witnessed organizational leadership that was stuck in survival mode because it was not guided by intelligent strategies. Without harmonizing strategy and leadership, organizations will continue to struggle. Any model that focuses on one without the other is destined to fail.

This book could not have been completed without significant contributions from a number of good people. I would like to acknowledge my amazing team at our independent boutique think tank the Cambridge Institute for Global Leadership, for their hard work in making this book happen.

I would also like to thank Marwa Itani, who spent three years diligently researching, and then translating the research, ideas, thoughts, and my experiences into the book you see before you. Furthermore, Roy Sayegh, who spent many days helping me refine my thoughts by asking me about the little nuances that define the PDG Model. Roy also was in charge of incorporating the enhancements of every new version.

Mary Shammas beautifully designed the cover and illustrations, and formatted the book. She also gave valuable comments on the content. Dr. Susan Murray and Adam Smith Albion reviewed the book twice, generously offering her insights, and Susan Simons added her usual elegant touches to the artwork of the cover, the illustrations, and the formatting. Karen Tallentire and Douglas Williams edited and polished early versions of the manuscript, and Jo Lavender deserves much appreciation for later edits of the book, which helped to maximize the reading experience.

I also thank my many friends and loyal readers around the globe for their feedback on the book and its production. Your encouragement keeps motivating my passion for sharing knowledge.

Last but not least, thank you, honorable reader, for choosing this book and for your support of our continued commitment to share with the world everything beautiful we've been taught by life, passionate work, and brilliant people.

I hope you enjoy the book.

INTRODUCTION

> »
>
> People should not be unfamiliar with strategy,
> those who understand it will survive, those who do
> not understand it will perish.
>
> *- Sun Tzu*
>
> «

I will respect your time and intelligence.

If you are reading this book, you are interested in strategy. You may or may not have read other books about strategy. Your work may or may not be predominantly strategic. I am confident, however, that like me, you have been bombarded by the word "strategy" over the past few years. Strategy appears in conversations about business, politics, and everyday life. Some people throw in the word to imply deep thinking and intellectual sophistication without necessarily meaning anything in particular.

Strategy is not about being profitable, earning higher market shares, being the best, being the biggest, winning, or increasing sales. These are just aspirations and hopes. Many organizations today concentrate on these things and fail, not because these things are bad, but because they become the sole focus.

By putting strategy in a wider context and redefining success, you can greatly improve your chance of excelling.

> A "bad strategy" is one that doesn't even try to address an important challenge. Instead, it speaks of aspirations, visions of the future, lays out performance goals, or simply lists a bunch of unconnected actions.
>
> *– Richard P. Rumelt*

This book aims not to discuss strategy as a standalone term, but to view it on a broader and more comprehensive level that also emphasizes leadership. I have learned that even the best strategy has little chance of success if it is not driven by intelligent leadership, which can see its way to execution in spite of existing and emerging challenges. Strategy without leadership is doomed, as is leadership without an adaptive strategy. This book should be considered, in some ways, a **hybrid of strategy and leadership**, because I have learned that **both are vital requirements for survival and growth.**

Strategy is a process that helps you to achieve what matters most to you and your organization. To be effective, it needs to be part of the larger framework of a growth mindset and a leadership model.

So, what is growth?

Some define growth as increasing market share, profit, customers, or even geographic reach. However, I choose to adopt a wider definition. I define healthy growth as holistic progress that benefits all stakeholders and generates sustainable financial gains.

In its simplest form, this definition applies to all types of organizations, from a bakery shop to a conglomerate, to a nonprofit organization, and even to a country. For instance, the higher the beneficial value of the goods and services the bakery offers, the more customers will come, and the more often they will return; hence, more profit will be earned. Note that when I refer to the customer, I mean anyone the organization aims to serve, not just those who spend money, so this also applies to nonprofit organizations, where the customer is the person they wish to help.

Increasing financial gains and creating value go hand-in-hand, and both are essential to growth. If you provide value that satisfies and helps individuals grow and prosper, you will have laid down the foundation for a sustainable organization. When people frequent a business, so does their money, and the resulting profits help the organization not only sustain itself, but also acquire more knowledge, provide more training, innovate, and grow.

>>

> The purpose of the corporation must be redefined as creating shared value, not just profit per se. This will drive the next wave of innovation and productivity growth in the global economy.
>
> – *Michael Porter*

<<

So, is your organization on a journey of growth?

That depends on your answers to the following questions:

1. Is your organization growing financially?

2. Is the well-being of the people in your organization improving?

3. Is your organization making great positive impact on the people that it is serving?

4. Does your organization follow a clear purpose and embrace an adaptive culture?

If the answer to all these questions is "yes," then ENJOY. Whatever you are doing seems to be working and you are on the right path. Remember to keep these questions in mind as you continue, and check if your answers change. You never know how the tides will turn.

If the answer to one or more of these questions is "no," then it might be a good idea to consider how to move out of an unpleasant reality, and instead start building one that fits your aspirations.

Some people find it difficult to admit to struggling with things, but a key to progress is to be open and aware of your strengths and weaknesses; only then can true growth occur.

A common reason companies fail to grow is that they rely heavily on logic and rationality, without factoring in a major characteristic of humans – emotions. **Many people fail to realize that emotions, not rational ideas, dominate in matters relating to humans,** whether these matters involve personal life, family, a business, an organization, or society as a whole. A considerable amount of our ongoing problems persist because decision makers avoid dealing with the emotional aspect – it is hard. Humans usually remember how something made them feel, not the specifics of the event, and it's crucial to bear this in mind.

»

I've never seen impeccable logic be sufficient to win both the heart and the mind.

– *Scott D. Anthony*

«

What does this human characteristic have to do with business? Organizations are populated by humans, each possessing tools to help the organization progress, or regress. Growth results not just from good planning or technical facilities, but also from the care and passion of individuals on the team.

I wrote this book because, through my education, I gained a deep understanding of what strategy entailed from some of the greatest minds on this subject – Michael Porter of the Harvard Business School and Ronald Heifetz of the Harvard Kennedy School of Government. In further education, I learned how strategy can be applied to public policy at the Woodrow Wilson School of Public and International Affairs at Princeton University. During my research, I examined the various schools of strategy. Among others, these include the:

- Design school
- Planning school
- Positioning school
- Entrepreneurial school
- Cognitive school
- Learning school
- Power school
- Cultural school
- Environmental school
- Configuration school

While these schools of thinking offer different perspectives on strategy, each with its own strengths, none of them have yet offered a comprehensive, holistic, practical, and realistic approach to strategy in a rapidly changing and volatile world.

Professionally, I have spent the past thirty years dealing with strategy from within the corporate world, and I wrote about strategy-related events for many years as a journalist for Reuters. In my career, I have worked in more than twenty countries, experiencing a variety of cultures and attending hundreds of meetings that revolved around strategy. During this time, I made many strategy-related mistakes. Each mistake offered me a valuable lesson that helped further my understanding of the concept. Of course, the learning journey is still ongoing.

Finally, the executive leadership programs that I organize and host have given me insight into the minds of thousands of business and government leaders, from middle management up to CEOs – even to heads of state.

From all these experiences, trying and testing different approaches to strategy, I have come up with a model that goes beyond just strategy, which I have packaged into a comprehensible and practical framework.

I believe the following model incorporates the right balance between the emotional and rational components, offering a holistic model for an individual or any kind of entity to sustain survival and achieve growth – the Purpose-Driven Growth Model (PDG Model). I will introduce the steps in the model now and elaborate on them further in the following chapters, with examples to make them clearer.

The Seven Steps of the PDG Model:

Step One: Define your uniqueness. What are you made of? The first step involves creating an inventory of your strengths. Each individual and organization has a unique composition and combination of knowledge, skills, experiences, and assets. This step is about being aware of and unlocking strengths.

Step Two: Define your purpose. Where could you have the most valuable impact? Using the inventory created in the first step, choose the aspect of your uniqueness which you feel can add the most value to those around you. How can you share the best parts of yourself in service of the world? How can your organization bring remarkable value to others?

Step Three: Design your strategy. What is your road map to fulfilling your purpose? What choices will you make? In this step, you create the blueprints to make your purpose, and your organization's purpose, come to life.

Step Four: Look inward. Are you prepared for the journey? Are there any internal barriers preventing you or your organization from implementing the strategy? Do you have the appropriate capacities, resources, processes, structure, and culture? This step builds your awareness of the internal obstacles and advantages. Are the individuals in your organization working well together? Is the environment one that prompts growth?

Step Five: Fix and prepare. Have you removed the obstacles standing in your way? Have you built the required capacities? This step is about removing the internal barriers, and reinforcing or acquiring the strengths that you identified in the fourth step.

Step Six: Execute brilliantly. What measures are you taking to ensure that your implementation is of the highest quality? This step utilizes your preparation, project management skills, problem-solving capabilities, and practical intelligence to successfully execute your strategy.

Step Seven: Remain adaptive. How are you adjusting to the changing seasons? Even with flawless execution and success, this step is crucial to maintaining success through constant innovation, learning, and adaptation. Even the most successful leaders and organizations need to refresh their knowledge and continue learning.

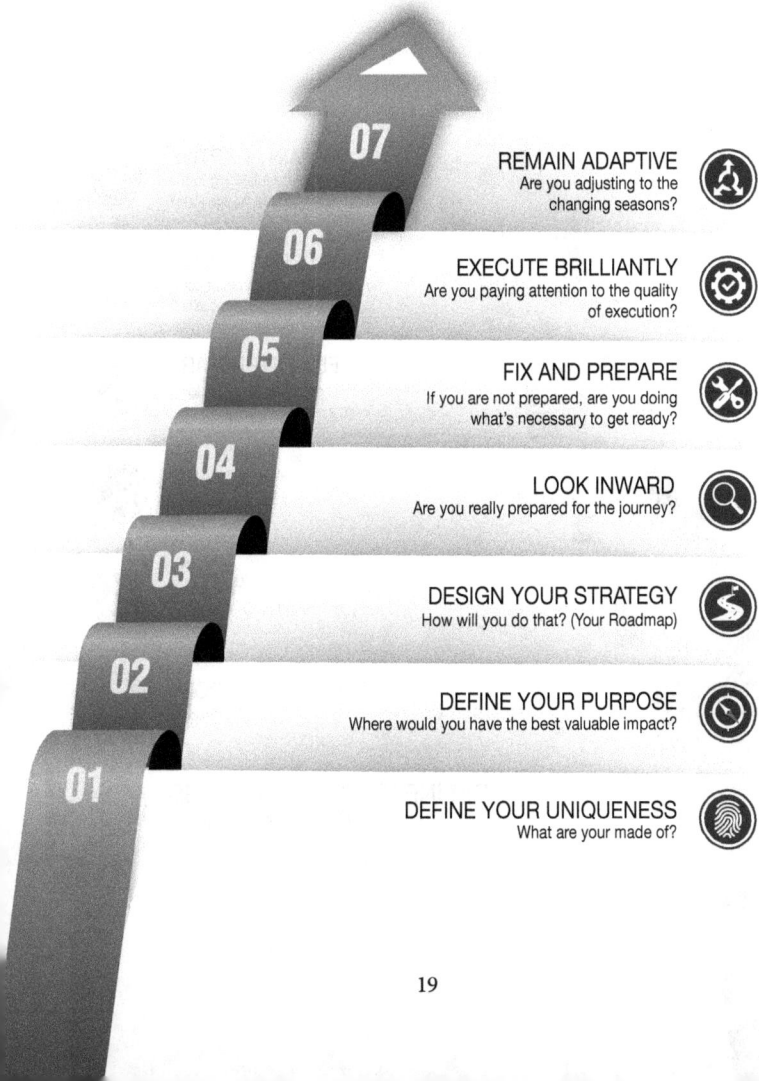

THE PDG MODEL

07 REMAIN ADAPTIVE
Are you adjusting to the changing seasons?

06 EXECUTE BRILLIANTLY
Are you paying attention to the quality of execution?

05 FIX AND PREPARE
If you are not prepared, are you doing what's necessary to get ready?

04 LOOK INWARD
Are you really prepared for the journey?

03 DESIGN YOUR STRATEGY
How will you do that? (Your Roadmap)

02 DEFINE YOUR PURPOSE
Where would you have the best valuable impact?

01 DEFINE YOUR UNIQUENESS
What are your made of?

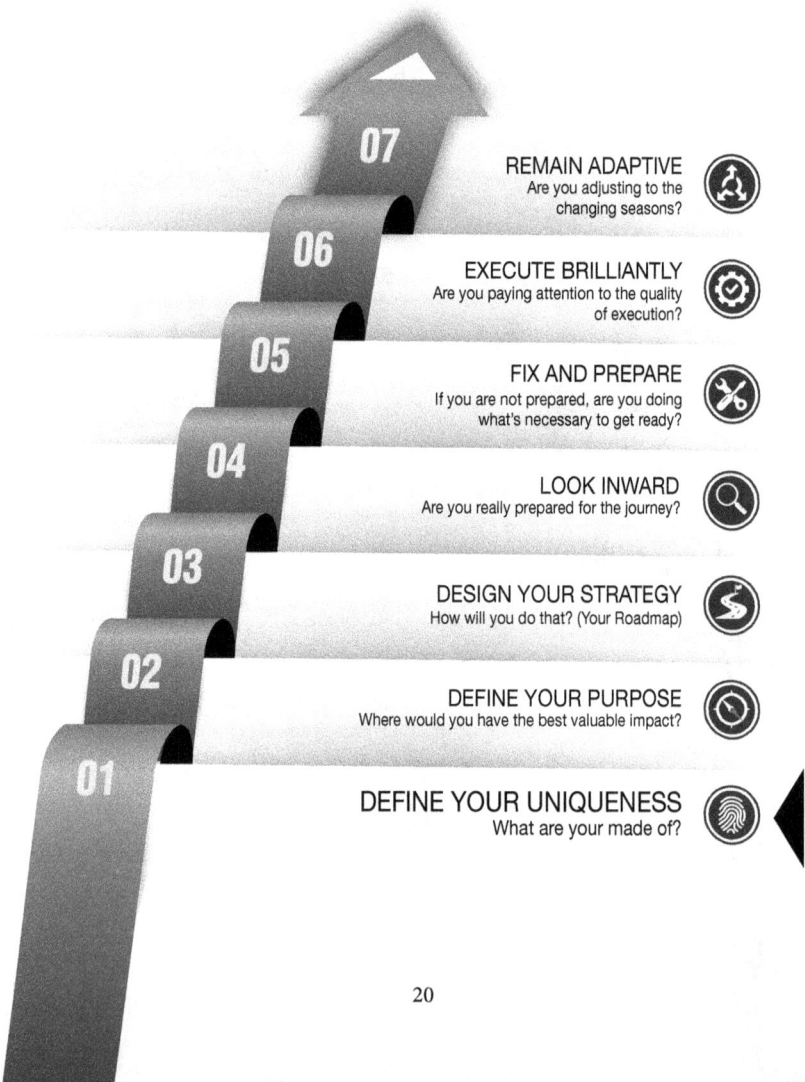

THE PDG MODEL

07 REMAIN ADAPTIVE
Are you adjusting to the changing seasons?

06 EXECUTE BRILLIANTLY
Are you paying attention to the quality of execution?

05 FIX AND PREPARE
If you are not prepared, are you doing what's necessary to get ready?

04 LOOK INWARD
Are you really prepared for the journey?

03 DESIGN YOUR STRATEGY
How will you do that? (Your Roadmap)

02 DEFINE YOUR PURPOSE
Where would you have the best valuable impact?

01 DEFINE YOUR UNIQUENESS
What are your made of?

CHAPTER ONE

DEFINE YOUR UNIQUENESS

> The essence of strategy is to create your own path.
>
> *– Michael Porter*

What are you made of?

This step is the most fundamental because it requires that you know yourself and your organization absolutely. Without this, the model has already **failed**.

How can you make decisions if you do not fully understand your capabilities?

We grew up hearing, "You're different; you're special," but when you ask people the simple question, "What makes you unique?" they almost always hesitate or respond with generic answers along the lines of "I am a CEO," "I am an empathetic person," "I have good communication skills."

We define ourselves as unique by the roles we play and our general traits, because very few of us take the time to look deep inside and discover our core selves. Many people would not even know where to start.

To discover your uniqueness is to understand your full capacity, your strengths and weaknesses. What does this mean?

In the general sense, we are all unique. This is a fact, and it's been true since the dawn of time. No two individuals are the same; every fingerprint is different. You as an individual will **NEVER BE REPEATED**. Every aspect of you, from your genes to your experiences, is unique.

I am, however, going to focus on one part of your uniqueness. Throughout this book, "uniqueness" refers to your inventory of qualities that contribute to value creation, ranging from your experiences and your preferences to your talents, acquired knowledge and skills, and personality traits.

For example, consider a person who suffers from an extreme phobia of germs (mysophobia). His routine and daily life center around avoiding germs. His routine is common, but his mysophobia makes him unique. Unfortunately, that uniqueness adds no value to those around him, aside from a spotless office, perhaps. However, if this person took his fear for germs to another level by becoming a passionate hygiene expert, studying all the different forms of cleaning products and devoting his time and effort to discovering the best ways to get rid of germs, he could add value to those around him.

On an organizational level, uniqueness may include the organization's resources, knowledge, culture, structure, or the special skills of its employees, etc., but not everything unique is included in the inventory. Only things that create value are.

For example, the fact that one employee loves music and plays the guitar may not add value to a law firm specializing in divorce cases, for musical talent is not particularly useful to the firm. On the other hand, if a case involved a singer who claimed that their ex-spouse copied a song of theirs, the employee with the musical background might be able to pinpoint the differences and similarities in both songs. Their uniqueness in this case would be of use. The list is flexible depending on the situation.

>>

Integrative solutions came directly from mining the existing models for the best of their nuggets. So I never start with a blank sheet of paper anymore.

– *Roger L. Martin*

<<

Uniqueness can emerge in many ways, such as through an innate talent (beautiful voice) or an interest (love for animals). Uniqueness can also arise from the experiences that shape us. For example, a mother loses her son in a car accident. Through this pain, she creates an organization helping teenagers and young adults drive safely, and devotes the rest of her life to this cause. This unique experience shaped what she became. Sometimes a single event defines your uniqueness. Furthermore, certain personality traits such as determination can be considered part of your uniqueness.

The uniqueness of some individuals is obvious from the start. For others, the process takes longer, as many parts of their personality traits and experiences come together to forge their unique strength. Effort and perseverance factor into one's uniqueness, since they are essential in reaching goals, regardless of one's raw talent.

For example, an individual who loves soccer and is determined to play professionally, but does not have talent for the game, should not give it up. **Those who truly succeed in any domain are the ones who have committed to their craft despite all odds.** Persistence and determination are not qualities all individuals possess and therefore they can be considered part of an individual's uniqueness, coupled with their love and passion for their craft. Although talent is an advantage, deliberate practice and devotion make a good player great.

A commercial that Michael Jordan did for Nike in 2008 draws out this illustration further. He says, "Maybe it's my own fault. Maybe I led you to believe it was easy when it wasn't... Maybe I led you to believe that basketball was a God-given gift, not something I worked for, every single day of my life."

Discovering uniqueness applies to an organization as well as to the individual. A start-up company must harness its uniqueness when deciding what kind of business to run.

For instance, an individual's love and talent for baking may have led him to practice and experiment in the kitchen, and he may then create unique cake recipes. Each element of this uniqueness – his love, talent, and experiences –motivates him to open his very own bakery shop.

Similarly, an established organization or company must look within and sketch out an inventory of their own uniqueness. Think about: what comprises your organization and what it's been through? What are the elements of differentiation that highlight your organization? How can these elements of differentiation be leveraged to create remarkable value and bring about growth?

Uniqueness vs. Competition

Build your business around your uniqueness and you never have to worry about competition

In today's world, most organizations forget about their uniqueness and strive to surpass their competition. Such rivalry is not inherently bad, unless it creates an overriding goal of beating the competition rather than focusing on what needs to be done to create value. This will lead organizations to compromise on quality. The "Jobs to be Done" theory proposed by Clayton Christensen supports this notion.

The theory states that, rather than just placing the customer first, **a company should understand the needs of the customer,** such as why the customer utilizes particular services or buys certain products. Understanding these reasons opens the door to more innovation, prompts alternate solutions to meet their needs, and further assists the customer. Focusing solely on outdoing the competition leads to short-lived wins and, often, a fixation on operational efficiency.

>>

Businesses want to think in terms of categories.
Consumers want us to think in terms of their needs.

– *Clayton Christensen*

<<

For example, consider two supermarkets competing head-to-head. One introduces a new product, so the other follows. They are entirely focused on outdoing each other, or at least on leveling the playing field, instead of focusing on distinguished value creation and truly serving the customer. The supermarkets may evolve until there is no difference between them, forcing customers to base their choice on convenience.

That dynamic will eventually drive the prices down, and profits will go down as well. The companies suffer, but so do the customers who now lack options, as they receive the same products and services from both.

The problem with competition arises when people use it not to differentiate, but merely to be "better," "bigger," or "brighter." **Perfecting existing techniques rather than innovating with something new and different limits creativity.** Organizations start measuring their success against the success of others, as opposed to measuring how well they have served their clients, whether they have created something of value, or whether they have improved on a personal or organizational level.

> »
> Strategy is about setting yourself apart from the competition. It's not a matter of being better at what you do – it's a matter of being different at what you do.
>
> *– Michael Porter*
> «

Please don't misunderstand me. Competition is not all bad. Strategic competition does serve two major purposes under the framework of uniqueness. It boosts your ability to learn from the mistakes and successes of others, to get a feel for what works and what does not. It also clarifies where you stand in terms of others, better defining your niche and making it easier to see how to differentiate yourself. Strategic competition helps you spot the chinks in your armor, and makes you realize what areas need to improve, or where you can be of unique service.

Nonetheless , it is time to shift your focus! It should not matter what others do. What matters most is focusing on your strengths and using them in the service of others to add value to their lives.

The first step in the PDG Model is about recognizing and becoming aware of the organization's uniqueness, then using it to achieve a competitive advantage. Remember, though, that uniqueness is not static; it grows with your experiences and as the acquired talent of your enterprise grows. Without recognizing or maximizing its uniqueness, your organization will get caught up in the frenzy of competition and aim at nothing more than replicating what is already out there.

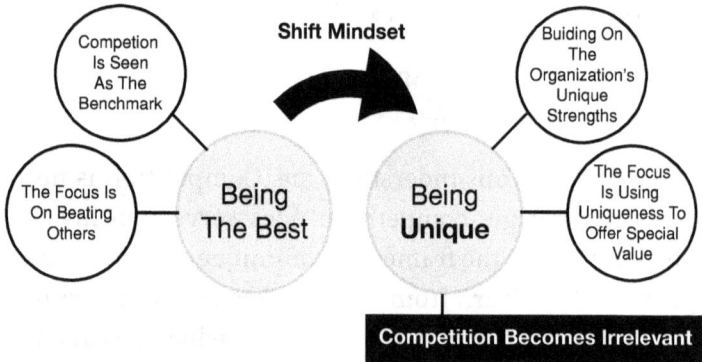

Figure 1.1:
Building a culture of uniqueness

Awareness Of One's Uniqueness

The concept of uniqueness is simple; discovering your uniqueness is not. It takes time and a great deal of introspection. It takes a deep level of awareness of the inner workings of your organization, and a thorough understanding of its strengths and weaknesses. You may be good at many things, but which activities truly add value to others? Keep in mind that uniqueness is rarely one characteristic or activity. **Often, it is the result of combining many common characteristics in an uncommon way.**

Uniqueness can be found in the many layers and interactions of your organization. For the sake of simplicity, your organization can be divided into two parts: the physical and the psychological.

On a physical level, what makes your organization unique? This can take many forms: geography, channels used, size, organizational structure, etc. This level includes all the operational activities of an organization.

On a psychological level, uniqueness can manifest in the diversity within the organization, the values the organization projects, the worldviews it promotes, and the culture it fosters. The psychological level includes the relationships and group dynamics within the organization , from the customers to the employees, to management, to authority figures, to other stakeholders (suppliers, shareholders, and the community). These are essential relationships that can make or break your success.

>>

In the end, an organization is nothing more than the collective capacity of its people to create value.

– *Louis V. Gerstner, Jr.*

<<

Uniqueness is the special blend of these components. Perhaps, on their own, each component seems fairly common, but the blend of them creates a unique synergy that no other organization will have. The truth is uniqueness does not have to be something big, bold, or obvious. It can be found in the simplest nuances that add to value creation.

For example, two stores may sell the exact same gifts, but customers choose one store over the other because of friendliness, the general homey feel of the place, and the way the customers are treated. Every facet, no matter how small or large, can affect why customers choose your organization.

Uniqueness is not fixed. With experience, individuals and organizations mature, dynamics change, and relationships alter. What made your organization unique five years ago may not endure today.

For example, Mozart had an innate talent for playing the piano, so he was unique as a young performer. However, his ultimate uniqueness as a composer matured after years and years devoted to perfecting his craft. Time changes things, and this can build upon the strength of your uniqueness, or even shift the focus of your uniqueness to new activities.

Let us consider an organizational example. Department stores and hypermarkets like Walmart and Target offered a diverse range of products at a low cost, and this set them apart from their competitors. However, this uniqueness was challenged by Amazon's ability to offer the same wide variety of products and services, sometimes at lower costs, on an online shopping platform with a convenient delivery method. The hypermarkets, department stores, and shopping conglomerates failed to adapt their uniqueness in time for them to maintain their customer base. As such, their uniqueness no longer adds the value it used to.

Questions

1. What are your organization's core strengths?

2. What is your understanding of the organization's strengths and weaknesses?

3. What is your organization's biggest success story?

4. What are the wisest business decisions your organization has made?

5. What's your organization's physical uniqueness (e.g. global presence, vast properties, most up-to-date technology in your industry/field)?

6. What unique skills do the members of the organization, including yourself, have?

7. How can the organization best serve your clients?

8. What can your organization offer customers that nobody else can offer in the same way? What need can your organization fulfill?

9. What unique solutions can you provide to solve your customers' major problems?

10. How can you build on the organization's strengths to create differentiation? How can you minimize its weaknesses?

11. How can you inject more care and value into what you do?

12. How strongly do your clients depend on you? Why?

13. What are you bringing to the table that is tailored to your customers' needs?

Uniqueness Sets The Stage

Essentially, uniqueness is a fundamental step in understanding what your organization is comprised of and where it fits in the bigger scheme of things. It will help you formulate the organization's purpose. This helps to guide future decisions, and keeps the strategy and execution focused. Uniqueness creates the inventory, listing the assets which are important for your organization to capitalize on.

The next step, purpose, looks at contribution and value creation: where should your organization put its focus to add value to others, as well as to make profit to sustain itself and grow? What can you use from your list of unique attributes to sustainably add true value to the world around you? What will your ultimate concern be?

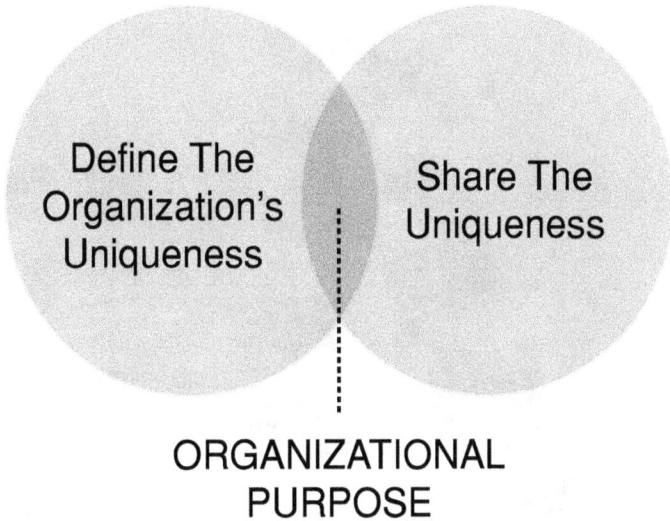

Define The
Organization's
Uniqueness

Share The
Uniqueness

ORGANIZATIONAL PURPOSE

Figure I.2:
Organizational purpose is about defining and sharing your uniqueness in a profitable manner

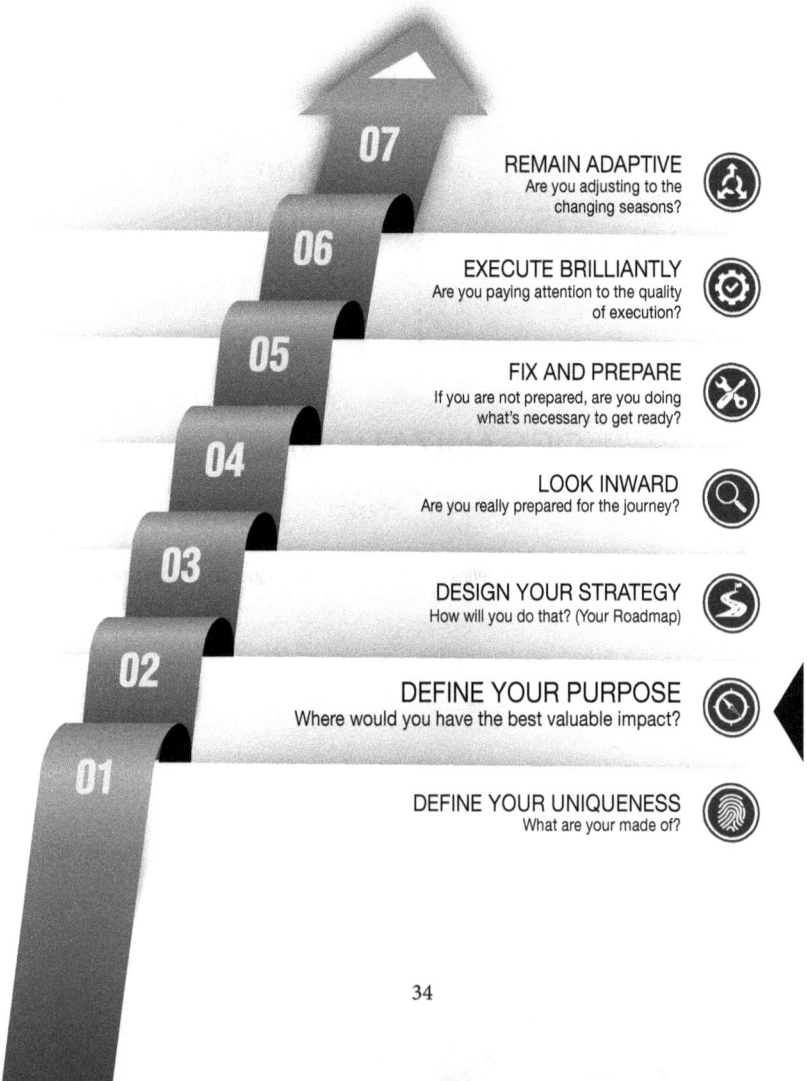

THE PDG MODEL

07 — REMAIN ADAPTIVE
Are you adjusting to the changing seasons?

06 — EXECUTE BRILLIANTLY
Are you paying attention to the quality of execution?

05 — FIX AND PREPARE
If you are not prepared, are you doing what's necessary to get ready?

04 — LOOK INWARD
Are you really prepared for the journey?

03 — DESIGN YOUR STRATEGY
How will you do that? (Your Roadmap)

02 — DEFINE YOUR PURPOSE
Where would you have the best valuable impact?

01 — DEFINE YOUR UNIQUENESS
What are your made of?

CHAPTER TWO

DEFINE YOUR PURPOSE

> Sound strategy starts with having the right goal.
>
> *– Michael Porter*

Where would you have the most valuable impact?

Why are you in business?

If "making money" is your answer to the question above then, with apologies to Monopoly, you will not pass GO, and you will not collect your $200. I am not saying that solely focusing on money is bad; I am saying it doesn't work. It will hinder your progress and prevent your business from becoming sustainable. If you want money, you must learn not to be fixated on it. Money comes as a result of creating value. Focus on fulfilling your purpose, and the money will follow.

What keeps a business alive and prospering is not
only making money, but touching the lives of your
customers in a wonderful way

Purpose is your WHY – why the organization does what it does; why you as an individual do what you do. Purpose provides the meaning beyond money.

Let's talk about sustainability. It refers to anything that keeps processes functioning and alive. To remain sustainable, you must make a positive contribution to the lives of people. This process certainly requires money, but sustainable inflow of money results from a focus on value creation. True sustainability only occurs when you improve the situation around you, offering something not commonly available – something people want to pay for. The bigger the value contribution, the longer it will last.

For example, if I sold a "revolutionary" shampoo, but when people tried it they discovered it was no better than other shampoos, how long do you think my product would last? Instead of focusing on how to make money alone, organizations should focus on providing the service or product that has great value and benefit. This will differentiate them from others.

To define your purpose, think about how you can solve a problem, or find an opportunity that creates value, adds beauty and knowledge, builds possibilities, and promotes abundance. These aims fulfill needs in society, and customers will reward you with appreciation, recognition, and long-term commitments of money and loyalty.

> If you keep your eye on the profit, you're going to skimp on the product. But if you focus on making really great products, then the profits will follow.
>
> *– Steve Jobs*

The Ultimate Purpose: Survival And Growth

Figure 2.1:
The ultimate purpose and drive of all organisms, human beings, and organizations is to survive and grow

The ultimate common purpose of all living organisms and systems is to survive and grow. This is built into the instincts of every organism. Without survival, there cannot be any continuity. Organizations are the same. The first aim of an organization is to ensure its survival, through finding a way to sustain itself and continue its existence.

Of course, there are instances where species become extinct. Usually the reason is that despite their drive to survive, at a certain stage they failed to adapt to a changing environment. In the case of organizations, those which do not adapt to the changing environment, or stop creating and providing value, will crumble.

Survival, however, is only the first step. Humans, and by extension organizations, aim to secure their survival so that they go beyond it and grow. Remaining in a state of survival was a concern for many millennia, when our basic survival needs (e.g. food, water, safety, shelter) were not guaranteed. Nowadays, people aim for more. It is not enough for people to sustain themselves. We are driven to grow, to become better, to realize our potential, and to find peace of mind, happiness, joy, fulfillment, etc.

Organizations also aim to grow, to become more profitable, to expand operations, to increase their customer base. Organizations are built to ensure that they are always moving forward and growing, finding ways to expand their presence. Usually, the way organizations can secure this state is by offering remarkable value to their customers, and trying to improve their well-being.

Organizations that focus on adding exceptional and unique value to their customers (value creation) will most likely secure their sustainability (survival) and move beyond it towards growth.

Purpose vs. Uniqueness

Purpose reflects your unique way of offering value to your customers

In the previous chapter, we discussed uniqueness as an introduction to the larger concept of purpose. Uniqueness is a crucial first step because you must know what your organization can offer and what it comprises of – the inventory of its strengths and weaknesses – to understand how it can provide unique value.

Purpose is what you choose to pay attention to. It is where your organization's uniqueness and value intersect with the needs of the world. It is deciding what you as an individual or organization excel at, what you **care** about most, and what **adds the most value to others.** You must also consider what aspects of the organization's uniqueness people care about enough to pay for. Purpose injects care and meaning into the equation. It makes your inventory of strengths meaningful .

Care is a driving force for sustainability and it allows

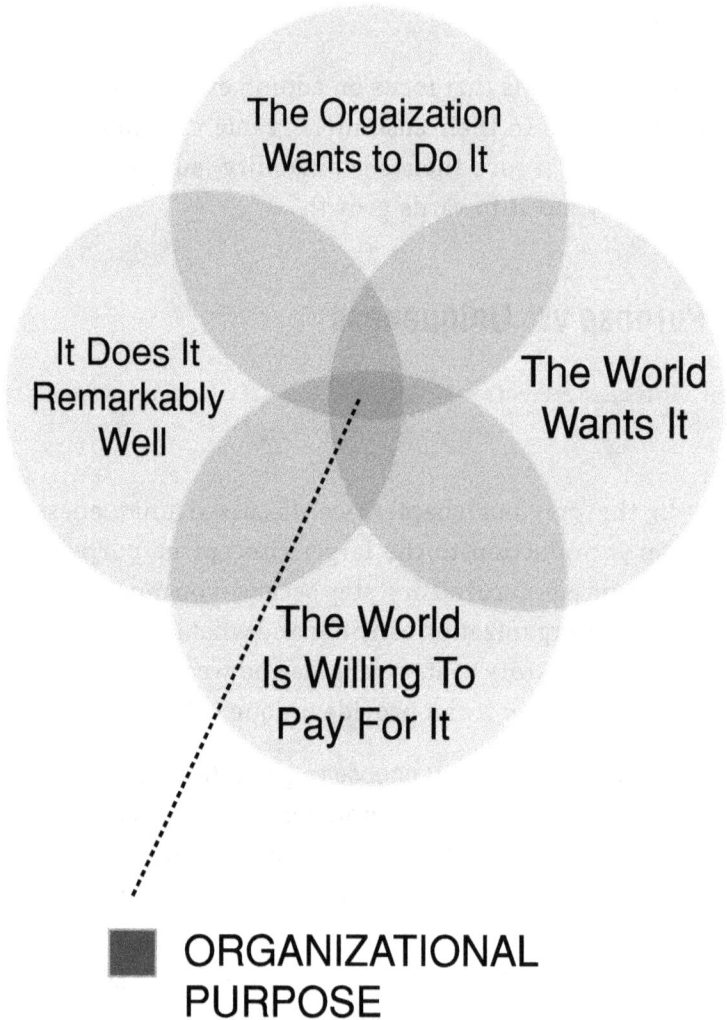

The Orgaization
Wants to Do It

It Does It
Remarkably
Well

The World
Wants It

The World
Is Willing To
Pay For It

ORGANIZATIONAL
PURPOSE

Figure 2.2:
The construction of organizational purpose

a person to focus on making a positive contribution. If the person does not care, commitment will be difficult to sustain. When times are rough, money only motivates people so far, but passion and meaning keep people going with or without financial reward.

>>

Give your employees a mission that matches their ambitions. When you challenge people, they surprise you.

– Richard Branson

<<

For instance, in the previous chapter's mysophobia example, the person used his uniqueness to become an expert in all forms of cleaning products. If he went on to create an effective cleaning product, the business selling that product could have the purpose of protecting living and working environments against harmful bacteria and viruses, and the person's uniqueness would match that purpose.

Uniqueness and purpose form two crucial steps in the PDG Model because they clarify your identity and guide the rest of the decisions you make. Sometimes these steps can be interchangeable, since uniqueness and purpose are often aligned, and the combination of the two adds great value to people's lives. It doesn't really matter whether you are driven by a purpose and adapt your uniqueness to fit it, or you are driven by your uniqueness and you use it to define your purpose.

It is the combination of these two steps that the PDG Model builds on.

Let us consider two examples which highlight the relationship between these two steps. For instance, a drug called *Minoxidil* was originally marketed as a medication for hypertension. However, over time, one of the common side effects was random hair growth. In response to this revelation, the company eventually gained FDA approval to sell a topical form of this medication to help with hair loss. In this case, the uniqueness of the medication defined its purpose, so uniqueness came first, followed by purpose.

In the reverse example, let's look at Maggie Doyne, the founder of the non-profit organization Blink Now, who visited Nepal when she was 19. After meeting an orphan and witnessing the harsh working conditions which orphans suffered to survive, she decided that she wanted to build a home for orphans and help to educate them. She used her life savings ($5,000) to buy a piece of land on which to build the "Kopila Valley Children Home". She continued to raise money to complete the home, and eventually she won an award of $100,000 to build a school (Kopila Valley School).

The non-profit organization she founded aims to help spread this purpose across the world. In this case, she defined her purpose, without any prior knowledge of how she was going to fulfill it, and then she set out constructing a strategy around this purpose. Her uniqueness as a young American in Nepal allowed her to effectively communicate with charitable organizations in the United States and successfully raise funds for her project.

Maggie Doyne established a purpose, and then looked at how to build uniqueness around that to ensure her organization offered maximum benefits to its stakeholders.

Regardless of whether purpose follows uniqueness or vice versa, the critical element for an organization's survival and growth remains offering a positive contribution to its beneficiaries.

If a product or service doesn't work – if it does not fulfill its purpose – then it provides no positive contribution. People will see no use for it, and it will not sell. Similarly, each organization needs to focus on its positive contribution to remain sustainable in our interdependent world. Of course, you'll be able to think of examples of products that do not actually work, yet survive and remain in stock because people are misled by advertising or there are no practical alternatives, but **no organization should aim at just surviving.** This book is about taking sustainability a step further, beyond survival, towards growth.

The reputation you gain from your exceptional product is, in the long-term, more valuable than the direct profit you make from it

Failed products may survive, but their companies

will not expand because they do not provide real value. People may use the product once and throw it away, ignoring it in the future because they know it does not work. That product's bad reputation will erode the company's reputation. Sustainability, therefore, happens only with true value, not just the illusion of value, and there must be enough value to convince people to repeatedly pay for that particular product.

Note also that, in many cases, products may share the same purpose, but are made up of different unique components. For instance, the two medications *Tylenol* and *Advil* both alleviate headaches (purpose), but their active ingredients (uniqueness) are different. Some people respond well to the acetaminophen in Tylenol; others respond better to the ibuprofen in Advil.

> A company can usually grow faster – and far more profitably – by better penetrating needs and customers where it is distinctive than by slugging it out in potentially higher growth arenas in which the company lacks uniqueness.
>
> – *Michael Porter*

In a company, unique components transform a product from average to great. They are the path to differentiation and growth. Many companies will copy products and maintain a functioning business, but this is not the recipe for an outstanding product.

For example, so many brands sell sugar that people

may not focus on the brand when buying the product, because the contents of the packets are essentially the same. However, adding uniqueness to the concept of sugar by selling it in small, convenient cubes offered something new. That simple difference in format transformed a common item into one that was easier to use in many situations, adding value to the customers and contributing to the organization's progress and growth.

The path to growth for an organization is either to fulfill a need with a completely new concept, or to improve on something already available. Why keep providing average products and services in an already congested market?

Purpose And Branding

I think the more important task for a young person than developing a personal brand is figuring out what she's great at, what she loves to do, and how she can use that to leave an imprint in the world. Those are tough questions, but essential ones. Answer those – and the personal brand follows.

– Daniel H. Pink

Branding provides another example of why it is crucial to understand a company's uniqueness and purpose. How can you brand your organization if you do not know its identity? We cannot brand an organization based on its similarity to others. It must have a distinguishing mark to differentiate it. You must provide a unified image to the outside world, but first this image must be clear to people working in the organization. Knowing your purpose is crucial.

An organization creates a brand to show the world what it stands for. A brand provides something for customers to associate with and learn to trust, approach, and even love. How do you get the people you serve to love you? According to American psychologist Robert Sternberg, love requires three elements: *passion, intimacy, and commitment.* Purpose can provide all three.

<u>Purpose provides passion</u> because people know that when they associate with this brand, they are associating with something bigger than themselves, something they consider a good cause, or something that adds value.

<u>Purpose provides intimacy</u> because, when an organization has purpose, its priority is its customers – those it serves. It concerns itself with what the customers need and how the organization can make their lives better. When the business focuses on improving customers' lives, it forges strong bonds with the customers and it builds loyalty and intimacy.

<u>Purpose provides commitment</u> because it maintains a level of consistency throughout the years. When your customers know your purpose, they can depend on the fact that you will not suddenly veer off track.

Purpose Is The Heart Of Any Organization

1. Do you know your organization's purpose?

2. Why does your organization do what it does?

3. What is the real and unique value that you offer to the people you serve?

4. Do your stakeholders know the purpose? Your customers? Your employees? Your suppliers? Your shareholders?

If you get a variety of answers when you pose these questions, or "I don't know" in response, you may need to reconsider how you have defined your purpose. You should also reconsider the direction of your organization, because this ought to be based upon your answers to these questions. Refocus your attention, return to the basics, strip away all the layers, and rediscover your fundamental core, your identity – or, as we have been discussing, your uniqueness.

Most organizations can tell you what they DO. They even know HOW they produce their products. However, as soon as you start asking them **WHY** they do it, things become confused. According to Simon Sinek's book, *Start With Why*, the truly inspiring leaders make sure others understand why they are doing what they do. The "why" is the core of any matter you pursue. It creates the only path to reach people at an emotional level, to speak to their hearts. Exceptional organizations usually have a clear purpose known by all.

In the 1980s, Steve Jobs stated that Apple's purpose statement was: "To make a contribution to the world by making tools for the mind that advance humankind". Disney's purpose was "To make people happy". These organizations knew their purposes. Does yours?

Purpose allows an organization to focus on making a positive, defined contribution, and it also **allows it to focus on value creation and impact.** Above anything else, customers want to know that the product or service is reliable, consistent, and performs exactly as promised. Purpose clarifies the goal for an organization, providing a framework that helps maintain the consistency and reliability of its products.

>>

Quality in a service or product is not what you put into it. It is what the client or customer gets out of it.

– Peter Drucker

<<

People do not buy an Apple iPhone only because it looks good, although elegant design stands as one of its greatest appeals. They buy an iPhone because they know they can depend on it lasting, because Apple has demonstrated that they produce consistently high-quality products.

Purpose gives organizations meaning; it appeals to a deep human psychological need. People will not be lured in by complicated high-tech services and products. These features may be important to the product, but they will not draw in the average customer. Customers are attracted to a product they can trust, created by an organization that understands their needs. Because the organization cares about its customers, the customers know the products they buy will work in a way that suits them. Similarly, an organization providing services focuses on offering genuinely effective, useful services that clients can depend upon to improve their lives.

This relationship breeds loyalty. When the organization demonstrates to its customers that the value offered by its products or services will not falter, its customers learn to depend on and trust the organization. This trust is cemented further when customers know the organization cares about more than just profits, and that it actually wants to continuously improve and provide them with increased value.

Purpose also energizes your employees, instilling them with a sense of meaning. People generally crave order and focus, and providing them with a clear purpose lends their daily activity meaning. They will understand what they are aiming to achieve, and will be better able to see the impact of their work and how it fits into the overall structure.

When you give employees meaning, you increase their motivation. They work harder, push more limits, and try their best because they believe that their work offers value – they are internally motivated. If they see their job as only a means to an end, focusing on external factors to motivate them (e.g. money), they will put in minimal effort. Do not underestimate the value of finding meaning, which can effect everything, including the company's bottom line. Purpose pushes us beyond our limits.

A clear and concise purpose unifies and mobilizes employees

When you give employees a reason to care about what they do, to genuinely see their work as meaningful, their output changes. They will start to sacrifice time and effort to vastly improve whatever your company offers. They will see a reason to do this beyond the financial motivation of their wages, because they will understand what your product is trying to achieve beyond bringing in profit.

>>

When there is genuine vision (as opposed to the all-too-familiar vision statement), people excel and learn, not because they are told to, but because they want to.

– Peter Senge

<<

Consider two people cooking a meal. One cooks just as a means to make food. The other cooks because he enjoys it, putting love and care into everything he does. Which meal do you think would look and taste better?

The same applies to services, products, or anything an organization means to do. When you get your employees to care about more than just their salary, you transform the time and energy they put into their work. This is passed on to customers, who can feel the value, just as the care in cooking would have been noticed by the person eating the dish. There is a palpable difference.

>>

It goes without saying that no company, small or large, can win over the long run without energized employees who believe in the mission and understand how to achieve it.

– Jack Welch

<<

1. What meaning has your organization brought to people? To its employees?

2. How do you communicate your organizations purpose?

3. To what extent do your customers experience your organization's purpose when they interact with it?

What Do Organizations With A Purpose Look Like?

>>

The secret of success is constancy to purpose.

– Benjamin Disraeli

<<

Purpose is real; it is not a fantasy concept. I am not here to sell you some romantic vision of you finding your true meaning. It's logical, clear, and necessary.

A survey conducted by the Harvard Business Review Team, called "The Business Case of Purpose," showed that 84 percent of executives believe that **an organization with a shared purpose would be more successful in introducing and implementing transformational changes.** Furthermore, it showed that companies with a clearly communicated purpose grew and transformed faster and more effectively than other organizations.

Organizations that focus on purpose are like people who stay calm amid a storm while others are lost or panicking. Purpose roots and grounds organizations, which makes it harder to push them down or throw them off course. Why?

Focusing on purpose simplifies and streamlines your decisions. When you know who you are and why you are doing something, you understand better what choices suit your needs. **The purpose becomes the benchmark you continuously reference.** How often does your organization use its purpose as a reference point when making important decisions?

The focus on purpose also increases trust, because purpose is about positive contributions, rather than just profits by any means. Employees and customers will more likely trust the company to follow through with its promises when they see that money is not the company's only concern.

Purpose also helps you weather storms and difficulties. If your mind is on purpose at all times, risks are easier to take, and mishaps easier to deal with, because you know where you're going. Purpose provides you with a basis for consistency without limiting your possibilities. It also helps you adapt to any storm that comes your way.

If you know your purpose, then you know in detail for whom the organization exists, who makes up your target audience, and how you will utilize your resources to better contribute to your customers and the community.

An organization with a purpose does not end with its founders; purpose breaks barriers, and is shared on all levels of the organization, from the employees to the suppliers. Purpose also breaks barriers between organizations. It is no longer about one business competing against the next; organizations work with each other for the benefit of the customer. Purpose helps organizations avoid *zero-sum competitions*.

>>

Purpose is not an add-on, it's not an initiative. It is a culture change and it never finishes.

– **Richard Branson**

<<

Here are just a few purpose statements from well-known organizations:

Nike: "To bring inspiration and innovation to every athlete* in the world." ("* If you have a body, you are an Athlete")

Tesla: "To accelerate the world's transition to sustainable energy."

Coca-Cola: "To refresh the world, to inspire moments of optimism and happiness, and to create value and make a difference."

IKEA: "To create a better everyday life for the many people."

Microsoft : "To empowere every person and every organization on the planet to achieve more."

Google: "To organize the world's information and make it universally accessible and useful."

Questions

1. Have you clearly formulated your purpose as these organizations have? If not, what are you waiting for?

2. What lessons can you learn from their actions? What can you take from their playbook to ensure your organization is purposeful?

3. How often does your organization act according to its purpose?

What Purpose Is Not

To help clarify what purpose is, let us understand what it is not.

The business world has been bombarded with numerous terms that organizations include within the framework of their businesses. Often, individuals confuse purpose with other business terms such as "strategy," "vision," "mission," "targets," and "values." However, these terms are not purpose and should not be used interchangeably with it. Each term is different and "purpose" is not just another word to add to the list.

Let's briefly go through them.

Strategy is the HOW, the practical choices that you must make to fulfill your purpose. It's about choosing **how to spend your finite resources,** and making decisions that will allow you to fulfill your purpose. For example, the ministry of education might choose to put a large portion of their budget into improving higher education facilities. The strategy is a decision that moves them towards their purpose.

Vision is what reality would actually "look like" once your strategy had been well executed, and your purpose had been fulfilled – it is a visual description of how success would be manifested. In the above example, the vision would be something like "having a university in every town or city of the country".

Mission is about accomplishing a task in the execution of the strategy. In the example above, the mission would be "building universities across the country."

Targets are defined milestones in the execution of the strategy. For instance, the ministry of education might set a target of "building one new university every two years in a different part of the country."

Values draw the boundaries for what is acceptable and what is not (much like a code of conduct). Purpose places our uniqueness in the service of others, whereas values set the boundaries of what is considered right or wrong while fulfilling your purpose. Your purpose should align with the values, but it is not a value itself. Values may include: equal opportunity, good governance, transparency, eco-friendly practices, etc.

The most important thing to understand about purpose is that **it is not a selfish endeavor**. Purpose is about focusing on improving the well-being of those you choose to serve, contributing to their lives in a positive and beneficial way – it is not about you. Purpose connects people in society, helping organizations and companies understand they are part of a bigger system. The more you contribute, the more you receive in return.

»

> If you study the root causes of business disasters, over and over you'll find this predisposition toward endeavors that offer immediate gratification.
>
> – *Clayton Christensen*

«

Reconnecting With Your Roots

If your company has survived decades and been successful, but recently encountered some turmoil, it's time to reconnect with what made you successful in the first place.

Many companies start off with a strong focus on their purpose. Companies like Wal-Mart and Ford began with purposes that revolutionized and changed lives. At times, however, companies veer from their original purposes. It is easy to forget what got the company going in the first place. As a company expands, unless there are constant reminders of its humble beginnings, it is increasingly in danger of forgetting its purpose in favor of profits and pleasing shareholders, etc.

This relates back to Clayton Christensen's concept: "Jobs to be Done," which discusses how organizations focus more on metrics related to their products than what the customer's actual need is.

So here are a few questions to get you back on track:

1.   Why does your organization exist?

2. Have you drifted away from your original reason for existence?

3. If so, how can you recapture that spirit?

Purpose And Strategy

Purpose is at the core of the PDG Model. Without it, organizations may shift their focus from value creation to profits and numbers. The meaning that purpose brings helps to ground an organization, and by extension it helps to dictate its decisions. Purpose offers up a framework and direction to create strategies that help to ensure the organization's continued survival and growth. In short, strategy – the next step in the model – is the choices that make your purpose come to life.

Questions

1. What opportunities can the organization create or take advantage of?

2. What are the top 3 things you do or sell that add incredible value for others?

3. What feature can you create that is missing in someone else's product or service?

4. How can you make the world a safer, healthier, more beautiful, more functional, and more engaged place while also being profitable?

5. What does your organization contribute to the community? What is your organization's image in the market? How can you improve it to better express the unique value your organization is creating?

THE PDG MODEL

07 REMAIN ADAPTIVE
Are you adjusting to the
changing seasons?

06 EXECUTE BRILLIANTLY
Are you paying attention to the quality
of execution?

05 FIX AND PREPARE
If you are not prepared, are you doing
what's necessary to get ready?

04 LOOK INWARD
Are you really prepared for the journey?

03 DESIGN YOUR STRATEGY
How will you do that? (Your Roadmap)

02 DEFINE YOUR PURPOSE
Where would you have the best valuable impact?

01 DEFINE YOUR UNIQUENESS
What are your made of?

CHAPTER THREE

DESIGN YOUR STRATEGY

> You need to be uncomfortable and apprehensive: True strategy is about placing bets and making hard choices. The objective is not to eliminate risk but to increase the odds of success.
>
> *– Roger L. Martin*

What is your road map to fulfilling your purpose?

Roll up your sleeves… this step is going to take a while.

Hundreds of books have been written about strategy. Companies like to flaunt it. It is one of the heavyweight words that gets tossed around, but how many people really know the true meaning of strategy?

Strategy has been given so much weight in the business world that it can sound intimidating, perhaps even overwhelming. Sometimes when we focus solely on strategy, we get stuck on trying to collect and analyze massive amounts of data, which can be paralyzing and overwhelming. Instead, if we choose to step back and take a bird's-eye view, we can see strategy from the perspective of our purpose, and the details may become less daunting.

As I see it, strategy is one step in the overall model rather than, as many seem to believe, the entire model . Strategy is the third step of the PDG Model because the HOW (strategy) becomes easier to formulate once you have identified your uniqueness and defined your purpose – the WHY – since the decisions must align with the purpose.

What Is Strategy?

>>

Strategy is about making choices, trade-offs; it's about deliberately choosing to be different.

– Michael Porter

<<

Strategy in its simplest form refers to the big choices you make in life.

Your strategy will dictate which road you will follow and how you follow it. Will you choose the road everyone is familiar with and run the risk of heavy traffic? Will you drive a huge truck to push aside the other cars? Or will you choose other roads that may not be safe, or that may be a little tricky to navigate, but which are quiet, untraveled routes?

You must decide who you want to be. Are you the driver who follows the crowd and waits behind everyone else? Are you the driver who ignores the rules, crashes into people, and continues on? Or are you the driver who finds another way to your destination, neither waiting behind others, nor harming them, nor being run over?

Strategy is about what you choose to do, and – just as importantly – what you choose NOT to do. It is macro-directional choices that emphasize who you are and how you fulfill your purpose.

Strategy takes your purpose and assigns concrete and tangible steps to it. It's your "Grand Plan." Without it, purpose would merely be an idea, and trying to execute your purpose would be like trying to construct a building without the blueprints.

Strategy is not a one-time choice. If you expect to set your strategy in stone, you will be unpleasantly surprised. The present does not stand still. The world is in motion, people change, surroundings alter, and so should your strategy. Therefore, your strategy can be considered your "best guess" in our ever-changing world.

Should your strategy be adaptive? Of course! Should your strategy change often? Probably not! It should change only when necessary and only in alignment with your purpose and the dynamic nature of your environment, within the limits of universal values.

How Do Strategy and Purpose Work Together?

Strategy takes your purpose and makes it real

An organization can, at any given time, be in one of four different states in relation to strategy and purpose:

Low Purpose; Low Strategy

This is where an organization is unclear about its purpose, and does not have a strategy. Such an organization is, at best, in a state of mediocrity. It may even be at risk of demise because the employees are indifferent. They don't know why the organization exists or how it wants to achieve its objectives. If a better opportunity presents itself they will leave, because no emotional connection ties them to the organization. To them, it is just a job that they do for lack of better options. Working in such an organization is often dull and lifeless, and lacking in creativity, productivity, and engagement.

High Purpose; Low Strategy

In this state, the organization has a clear purpose but does not have any idea how to fulfill it. The members of this organization are motivated but lost. They know the reason for the organization's existence, they are passionate about what they do, but they have no idea how to do it. If an organization in such a state does not develop a clear strategy quickly, motivation will diminish, and the organization may slide into a state similar to the previous scenario. As a result, it will lose some of its best members due to frustration.

Low Purpose; High Strategy

An organization in such a state usually has a highly bureaucratic culture where people are asked to strictly follow plans, processes, policies, and procedures without knowing either the purpose of the organization or the meaning and significance of their work. Employees in this situation will be technically active and busy, but emotionally disconnected. For them, the work is either about money or professional security.

High Purpose; High Strategy

In this state, people know why the organization exists, and they derive personal meaning from their work. They know how to fulfill the organization's purpose and add meaningful value. Of course, this is the ideal state for your organization to be in. Your people will be engaged, excited, passionate, focused, creative, innovative, resilient, persistent, motivated, and caring. The purpose of leadership is to keep the organization in this state of being, regardless of the changing external and internal conditions.

Questions:

1. Considering the above states of being. Where does your organization fit?

2. Is this your personal assessment, or is it shared by most of the people in your organization?

3. What should you do to move your organization into a state of High Purpose; High Strategy?

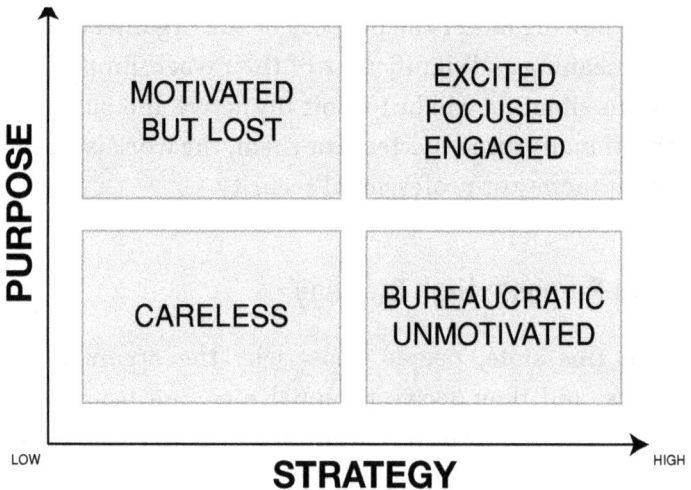

Figure 3.1:
The four states of being of an organization

Choices, Choices, And More Choices

I will go over the concepts of strategy briefly, because my goal here is not to explain strategy, but to show where strategy fits in the more holistic approach set out in the PDG Model.

The strategy (or the How) is the part in the model where you decide what industry you will choose, what services or products you will provide, who your clients will be, where your business will be located, what channels you will use to reach the clients, and how you will develop your capacities to get there.

Should you be a small boutique on the corner, or do you have enough resources to challenge the large conglomerates? Do you want to sell shoes, make-up, ties, or perfumes?

Strategy narrows down the options and makes your choice. You can't be everything, so what do you want to be? These are the kinds of questions required for developing strategies.

What I want to emphasize is the component that many organizations leave out: how does my choice support my purpose? What are the ultimate reasons for following this specific path?

This questions are as important as deciding what product to sell, or service to provide. Purpose anchors a good strategy, making it clear which options are acceptable and which are not. Your purpose marks out certain criteria or reference points that strategies should adhere to.

> »
> You can talk all you want about having a clear purpose and strategy for your life, but ultimately this means nothing if you are not investing the resources you have in a way that is consistent with your strategy.
>
> – *Clayton Christensen*
> «

Types Of Businesses

Businesses can take different shapes, sizes, and forms.

Some, unfortunately, are already dead. They have hit the last bump in the road, and declared bankruptcy. They await only the liquidation process.

Other businesses don't really have minds of their own. They are on life support, doing whatever it takes to break even, or pay off this year's bills. They still have the basic cash flow from somewhere or someone, but the core problems are neglected and nothing is changed. Money, slowly dissipating each year, functions as life support for a prone body. However, there is still a chance of rehabilitation and recovery if the brain wakes up.

At a higher level, but still in trouble, are those businesses that are bleeding. They have been lacerated in multiple places. They know they are sinking, but they aren't pursuing the right strategies to tackle the issues that have caused the bleeding. They are injured and instead of seeking help, they plummet downward until eventually, they join the other businesses in the fiscal version of death: bankruptcy, no resources, no options. Money talks, as they say, but in this case, it only says goodbye.

The next level is mediocrity. This might be a business making the choices to remain sustainable and break even, but not really offering anything new or different. It's the small grocery shop that you go to, not out of loyalty or because there's anything special about it, but for convenience. Such businesses sell the necessities – nothing different or unique – but they break even and make a little cash on the side to sustain themselves.

Next is the business that decided to open because it saw another one that was profitable and decided to follow in its footsteps. This business mirrors any other of its type, and could be described as reasonable, but nothing special. It is involved in a bit of competition, maybe by selling things at a slightly lower price than similar stores. At the end of the day, its strategy is to be like everyone else.

What about the business that focuses on profit only, where the motto is 'Show Me The Money!'? This business is always hungry for more money, more efficiency. The strategy is to run the business at maximum efficiency, try to lure in customers, crush the competition, and focus on financial growth at any cost, maybe sometimes compromising values and crossing ethical lines.

This business is always running – running after more, never stopping, and eventually the employees burn out and become resentful. The business is consumed by its appetite for speed and short-term accumulation of wealth. Such companies may have a high turnover rate because they don't slow down to breathe. Although they can operate for quite some time, they will eventually reach a breaking point as they compromise quality for higher profits and want everything done yesterday. All that matters to this type of company is that there is money in their pockets, for now at least.

Finally, there is the option I hope you will choose, though many do not. This is a company that follows a purpose and focuses on making a difference in people's lives. Examples could include not only big organizations, but also a local plumbing company that devotes itself to providing great services and building customer trust. The difference in quality is evident because they focus on their purpose, not just on making money.

What kind of company or organization do you want to be? Your decisions matter and may be the difference between expansion and bankruptcy.

Ask yourself:

1.   What kind of organization do I want to build?

2.   What is it that the organization would like to achieve?

3.   If the future could go my way, what would my organization look like? What activities would I be doing?

What Strategies Are Not

> The worst mistake – and the most common one – is not having a strategy at all. Most executives think they have a strategy when they really don't.
>
> – *Michael Porter*

To better grasp what strategy is, you need to understand the boundaries, and realize what strategy is not.

Most companies think they have mastered the concept of strategy, and therein lies the problem. Statistics presented by a study on strategies across the globe (conducted by A.T. Kearney in 2014) suggested that fifty percent of corporate strategies fail to meet expectations. Shocking? Not really.

Here are some common areas of confusion to examine. Strategies are **NOT**:

- Just a way to make money
- One size fits all
- About being everything at once
- Overly complex brainteasers
- Flights of fantasy

- Privileged information
- Constantly changing
- Etched in stone
- Mere attempts to improve overall efficiency
- A free-for-all

>>

As with the word "strategy", it unfortunately can mean a lot of different things to different people.

– *Michael Porter*

<<

Just A Way To Make Money

We keep coming back to this issue because it is a big one.

The business world has an increasingly negative reputation; people are less trusting of businesses, believing that businesses are driven by greed and just want their money. Imagine instead that businesses and strategies actually put customer well-being at the heart of their decision-making process, intending that their products or services should ultimately make customers happier and fulfill their needs. Customers would form a better relationship with businesses, and this would change the image that the business world has been suffering from.

I am not downplaying the importance of money; it is

essential for sustainability. I am merely suggesting that money will be abundant when you stop solely focusing on it, and **because** you stop solely focusing on it. The logic is that when you focus on making customers happy, contributing true value and worth to their lives, they will notice and will be appreciative. They will show their appreciation through loyalty and long-term commitment to your products and services, which is the key to sustainability. Research even shows that companies that focus on purpose are significantly more profitable than those that do not.

According to Joey Reiman's book, *The Story of Purpose: The Path to Creating a Brighter Brand, a Greater Company, and a Lasting Legacy*, companies driven by purpose outperform most services and products companies in similar categories by as much as 1,025 percent.

Of course, there are many organizations that do not provide a positive contribution and are still profitable. Organizations such as carbonated beverage companies and fast food chains arguably do not provide a net positive addition to the lives of individuals, given the health issues involved with their products. Despite this, they are some of the most successful businesses out there. However, here is an important observation: with customers' growing awareness of these shortcomings, these companies are slowly changing their ways. Pepsi-Co states that it has changed the menu of its beverages and even started to introduce some healthy options (e.g. water), and food chains such as McDonald's have also begun improving their menu to offer better choices.

So, there are many ways to make money. You can do it illegally, or you can do it by preying on the weaknesses of people, adding to their list of "needs," but even if the business is successful for a time, when customers start to realize their wants are not their needs, the business must adapt or die. **The PDG Model is based on holistic growth, not just profits. Growth only occurs through positive contribution and moving forward.** Why not pick a third option by making money through genuinely helping people?

>>

Profit for a company is like oxygen for a person. If you don't have enough of it, you're out of the game. But if you think your life is about breathing, you're really missing something.

– Peter Drucker

<<

One Size Fits All

Unfortunately, we can't just slap one strategy on all types of businesses, otherwise I would write the brilliant strategy for you right now and tell you to go forth and be successful. Each business has an intricate pattern that requires understanding the environment and weighing up all the factors in order to create its own unique strategy. Different situations and scenarios within the same organization also require tailored strategies.

About Being Everything at Once

> You cannot be everything to everybody, no matter the size of your business or how deep its pockets.
>
> *– Jack Welch*

Some businesses can get over excited; they want to be a gym, a diet center, and a day care all at once. It doesn't really matter how many things you do, but it matters very much how well you do them, and nobody can be everything to everyone.

A strategy requires choices, and this means ruling out some options. Part of perfecting a craft or providing a great service is knowing how to use your time and effort. If you stretch yourself too thin and try to do too many things at once, you won't complete anything properly.

For example, when Steve Jobs returned to Apple in the late 1990s, he made the critical decision to abandon 70% of the products the company was producing at the time. He felt that they were unnecessary and were merely an attempt to tailor products to retailers' requests. That critical decision to limit the products, abandoning dysfunctional ones, helped the company secure the success it enjoys today.

Overly Complex Brainteasers

Your strategy does not have to include everything. It does not have to consider the weather forecast and every minute detail of what may go wrong. The strategy needs to be **simple and easy to communicate**. The more complicated a strategy is, the more it risks miscommunications, misunderstandings, and something going wrong.

> Simple messages travel faster, simpler designs reach the market faster and the elimination of clutter allows faster decision making.
>
> *– Jack Welch*

Flights of Fantasy

You must be realistic about your strategy; think about time frames, consider your resources and capabilities, plan for delays and mistakes, and understand your limitations. All the expectations should be grounded in reality.

Ambition and optimism are traits to be admired, but make sure that your "grand plan" does not set you and your employees up for disappointment. You will become discouraged and may abandon your idea entirely.

Privileged Information

Your strategy is not top-secret or confidential. Sometimes it, or parts of it, should be kept secret from people outside the organization, but overall, most people inside should know what it is so they can work accordingly. The strategy needs to be communicated and understood, so that most people are on the same page and working in unison. This will direct behavior, but also motivate people as they understand the plan and what direction the organization wants to take.

Constantly Changing

> Strategy must have continuity. It can't be constantly reinvented.
>
> – *Michael Porter*

Although a strategy should adapt and change when necessary and remain in line with the purpose, changing too much can confuse people. You need continuity and trust. If you keep changing what you do or how you do it, you will lose both clients and employees to chaos. You can't be selling fruit juice one day and selling shoes the next. The strategy must be consistent, as this breeds trust, which is essential for growth.

Etched in Stone

The other extreme is also wrong. You cannot have your strategy etched in stone, immovable and unchanging. If it is, you will soon realize that the world has moved on while you're standing still. It is **crucial** for the strategy to remain adaptable, and this cannot happen if you believe the strategy is set in stone.

Mere Attempts To Improve Overall Efficiency

Strategy aimed at growth focuses on more than just being efficient. Efficiency alone may help your organization survive, but it does not ensure growth. A strategy that aims towards advancement as well as sustainability must go beyond efficiency, combining it with innovation, purpose, value creation, and other factors. **The solution to a problem is not always to work faster**; the solution can come from creativity and differentiation. Efficiency should not be the only means of differentiation; it won't sustain growth.

»

There is nothing so useless as doing efficiently that which should not be done at all.

– Peter Drucker

«

A Free-For-All

Strategy does not mean those in charge make up rules

on the spot. Constantly changing standards only create confusion. Each individual should have a clear and coherent role. That way, when a task is not completed or something fails, the source of the problem will be evident. There must be accountability and proper reward systems, which need to be clear, focused and well-known to all. Strategy demands increased coherency and understanding.

Making Sure You Make The Best 'Best Guess'

>>

Strategic thinking rarely occurs spontaneously

– Michael Porter

<<

Albert Einstein expresses this beautifully: "If I had an hour to solve a problem and my life depended on it, I would use the first 55 minutes determining the proper questions to ask."

Before making major decisions, it is imperative to **ask the right questions!**

Environment Analysis

1. Have you assessed your environment well?

2. Who has the power? Who are the big fish in town? Suppliers? Buyers? End consumers?

3. What are the general opportunities and threats in the external environment?

4. Have you assessed government regulations?

5. Is the area you have chosen politically stable?

Industry Analysis

1. What are the current conditions of your industry? How attractive is it? How intense is the rivalry? How high are the exit barriers? What about the entry barriers?

2. What markets/industries do you believe your business can offer the most value in? Are they narrow or broad?

3. What is the geographic scope of your organization? Is it local, national, or global?

4. What geographic markets (countries, regions) should you be in? Why are the markets you have chosen the most relevant? Are there any other markets that would be more beneficial? Which ones?

Competitor Analysis

1. If you were to make a list of your competitors, who would you include? Who will see you as their competition?

2. What are their strengths and weaknesses?

3. How good are their products and services?

4. How good are their innovations?

5. How aggressive is their sales activity?

6. How much does their culture emphasize the importance of growth?

7. What are they doing strategically and operationally better than you? What are they doing worse? What can you learn to do differently?

8. What have they done recently to gain a competitive advantage?

9. Have any of them introduced any innovations?

10. Have any of your competitors only recently entered the market? What have they been doing in the past year?

11. How will your competitors react to your new product/ service? How will you be able to deal with their reaction?

12. Are you limiting your strategy to a head-to-head competition with the strongest contenders? Are you copying their practices?

Internal Assessment

1. What are your main intentions behind offering your product/service? Is it solely to make money? Does it **benefit** others?

2. What resources support or constrain your actions?

3. Have you recently made any new acquisitions, created new innovations, or hired new talent?

4. Have you lost any key aspects in your business that previously gave you a competitive edge?

5. How are you getting to know emerging social and technological trends? What trends are observable today? How adaptive are you to future trends?

6. What can you do to shape these trends instead of adapting to them as they occur?

7. How can you give yourself an advantage over the current forces?

8. Have you explored all the different options?

Think carefully about the above questions, and make notes on your answers if necessary. This process should be carried out diligently because committing organizational resources to the wrong macro choices might be painfully expensive (in terms of finances and other resources).

It is important to dig a little deeper, even if at first an industry or market does not look attractive, or you feel it will be difficult to adapt to. You may be surprised to find that with the specific niche or special services you can offer, there is a place for you after all.

You must understand the needs of your environment. For example, when Home Depot opened a branch in China in 2006, it was not successful because they did not understand the environment that they were catering for. One of the major mistakes they made was the fact that Home Depot wanted to sell Do-It-Yourself solutions in a country where labor was so cheap that most people would opt to hire a handyman.

Assessing the environment includes understanding issues such as the political situation. Would you open a business in a politically unstable area? The opportunities available to you and the mentality of the people and their needs are both critical to understand. Selling items that require a speedy internet service in a country known to have slow networks would probably fail.

Legal factors can also be an issue. Will you encounter problems if you open a poultry feed business in an area zoned to exclude farm animals? Some areas have higher taxes, but there might be other pay-offs for being in these locations. It is important to weigh all the factors before making a decision.

> Strategy is, in essence, problem solving, and the best approach depends upon the specific problem at hand. Your environment dictates your approach to strategy.
>
> *– Martin Reeves*

We base the decisions we make on our "best guess", which is composed of three parts: all the relevant information that you can practically collect, your interpretation of this information, and what your intuition tells you.

Unfortunately, it's impossible to take every factor

into account and understand how each scenario will play out – nobody can predict the future. Sometimes intuition must drive our decisions, but this intuition should always be guided by the thorough understanding of the situation that an individual or organization is facing. Intuition cannot be a substitute for doing your homework and knowing as much as you can before you progress.

»

The only thing we know about the future is that it will be different.

– Peter Drucker

«

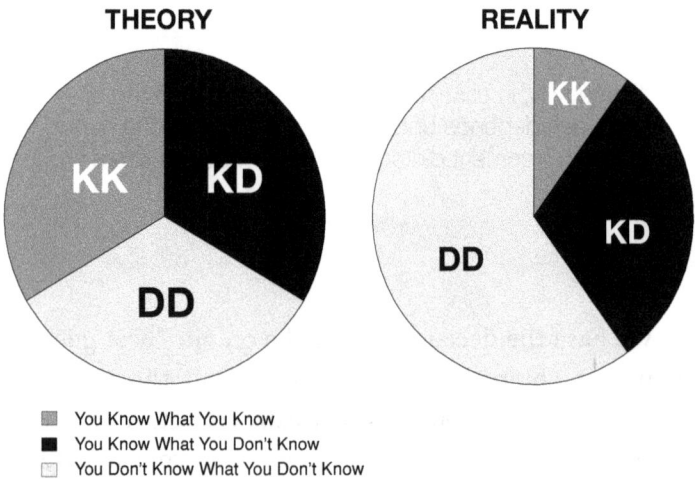

THEORY

KK KD

DD

REALITY

KK

KD

DD

▨ You Know What You Know
■ You Know What You Don't Know
☐ You Don't Know What You Don't Know

Figure 3.2:
Certainty/Uncertainty of knowledge

You may be thinking this is nothing new; you have heard it all before. However, knowing and doing are sometimes two different things, and oftentimes big mistakes happen because people fail to adhere to the fundamentals of sound thinking. Even experience does not outweigh looking at the environment and adjusting to suit it. You might be surprised how many presidents, CEOs, and business owners forego analysis of the environment, pushing through because they believe their instincts will be enough to carry them as they have in the past.

It is imperative to keep a balance between collecting information and paying attention to intuition. You cannot rely on either fully. You must research enough to get a good sense of what you are dealing with, and the rest must be open to adaptation as needed.

Let's remember what happened to companies like Kodak, Olivetti, Singer, and Polaroid.

Planning The Strategy

Nature Of Your Customers

1. What type of customers does your organization serve? What are their needs?

2. What things have customers been requesting that you've yet to deliver?

3. How will you reach your customers? What channels should you employ? Why?

4. What do you envision the future needs of your customers to be in 5-10 years, and how do you expect to meet them?

5. Which buyers might you have previously overlooked? Do you want to include them? How?

    •   Who purchases your products/services out of necessity rather than loyalty, and might be easily lost to your business? Do you want to reach out to them to ensure they remain your customers? How?

    •   Who refuses to use your industry's offering (someone who has seen the industry's offerings as an option to fulfill their needs but has deliberately decided against them)? How can you change their minds?

    •   Who might not have thought of the market's offering as an option to fulfill their needs? How can you access and attract them?

Competition

1. What are your competitors offering that may threaten your business (e.g. cutting-edge technology)?

2. What can you learn from looking across **alternative industries** (and not only looking at rivals within your own industry)?

Competitive Edge

1. What is the nature of your business? Does it provide a product or service of unique value, or is it more like a commodity? Are you growing as you should

be? What parts of your business are both profitable and add value to your customers?

2.   What can you bring to the table that would be **tailored** to your customers' needs?

3.   Why do customers do business with you? Why do they do business with your competitors?

4.   In what way can you frame your value proposition to encourage your customers to choose your business over your competitors?

5.   What innovations are in the pipeline that can help give you a competitive edge? Which ones will let you create a niche in the market?

6.   What product lines/services should you focus on? Why?

7.   Which organization offers products/services that are **complementary** to your own? How are they affecting you and what can you do about this?

What To Stop Doing

1.   What part of your business is "bad business" (one that is not aligned with your purpose and is not profitable)?

2.   What products/services should you discontinue?

3.   Which customers should you willingly let go of?

These feasibility studies and questions do not enable you to control the future; nor are they supposed to trap you in endless planning cycles. They are merely your homework, helping you understand and adapt to potential changes. Keep in mind that there will be unanticipated hiccups along the way. Although we love to think things will happen smoothly and without problems, there are almost always unexpected results.

»

In preparing for battle I have always found that plans are useless, but planning is indispensable.

– Dwight D. Eisenhower

«

You must recognize that there will be risks and uncertainty, as with most things in life. Some people try to plan for everything, try to predict and avoid risks at all costs. Though it is good to plan extensively, you should keep in mind that plans won't get you through every difficulty you face. Sometimes, when plans are compared with the reality they were intended for, you may find the options are narrower or less clear than you anticipated.

Sometimes you must make uncomfortable decisions. You may need to cut staff or rearrange your priorities, but when changes are necessary, you must have the courage to implement them. Always keep your purpose in mind.

Your strategy should be detailed enough for functionality, but not so detailed as to leave no breathing room for new ideas

The best planning creates a framework and understands the core elements of the plan, but leaves room for adaptations. Sometimes you won't know what you're doing until you get there.

When you have a foundation of information, be prepared to take risks. Do not hide behind creating further plans, but nudge people out of their comfort zones. To grow, you must strive to move away from the comfortable.

»

The best strategy is a balance between having a deliberate one, and a flexible, or emergent strategy.

– Clayton Christensen

«

Strategic planning may call for creative and unconventional thinking. Your organization will need to consider what novel practices, tools, and ideas can be introduced to increase its chances of success. Some of the ideas may fail, while others will succeed.

Here are three vital questions to keep in mind before making important decisions:

1. Is it in line with the purpose?

2. What is the cost?

3. Is it really worthwhile?

The Three Zones

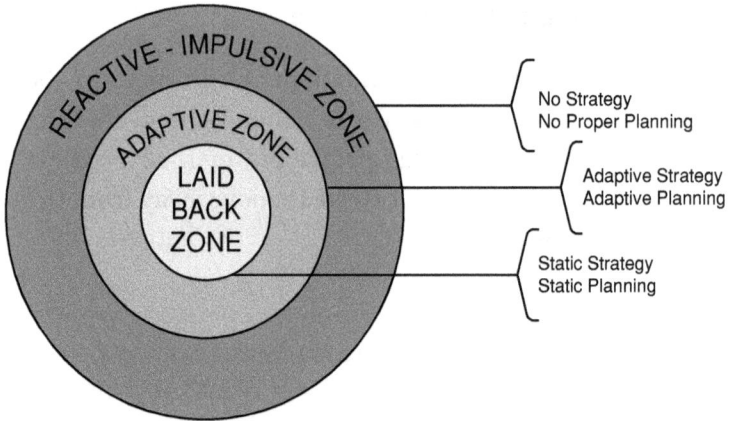

Figure 3.3:
The three zones of attitude towards strategy

Picture three zones: the laid-back zone, the smart zone, and the reactive-impulsive zone.

Staying in your laid-back zone means you don't try anything new. You regurgitate tried and tested methods that keep you exactly where you are. You will be stuck in the planning phase, reluctant to take risks and implement your strategy.

In the smart zone, you try new things, but you act rationally. The smart zone means you have spent some time planning, but you remain open to learning as you progress your plan. You adapt to the changing environment.

You are in trouble when you ignore plans or stop planning, and instead make impulsive decisions without a clear direction. In this case, you will have entered the reactive-impulsive zone. Without a plan you will be unable to function. You may experience debilitating stress, lacking the proper framework or strong foundation to help you through difficulties.

The First Three Steps Are Connected

Strategy is about how you choose to use your uniqueness to fulfill your purpose

The first three steps of the PDG Model – uniqueness, purpose, strategy – are undoubtedly intertwined. At any point during those three steps, you must be ready to ask yourself whether you are providing something unique or different. Does each added layer and activity increase the value of the entire model? If not, take it out.

Keep in mind that, while you may be successful in a given moment, if you are not continuously trying to improve your craft while staying true to your purpose, you could start to drift backwards. It is imperative that you choose each activity carefully and constantly check whether you are improving.

Ask yourself the following questions:

1. What activities do I provide that are considered remarkable?

2. What activities are lacking?

3. Which activities should be taken out because they only pose a hindrance?

Let us consider an example to ground these questions. In an upscale hotel that targets wealthy middle-aged people, they have a restaurant that is the talk of the town. The experience is exquisite, and it is often booked months in advance (this is their activity that is considered remarkable). On the other hand, it does not have a spa, even though its tenants come to relax. The hotel may need to consider adding this activity that they are lacking. Finally, they have a nightclub, but it is noisy, disturbing the tenants' peace and worsening the overall experience. This activity often causes complaints from the tenants, and affects their chances of returning for another visit.

If it is hard to reduce activities or make decisions, imagine the following scenario. If you had half the resources or staff that you currently have:

1. What would you focus on?

2. What would the most important activities be – the ones you deemed indispensable for your organization's survival and growth?

3. Why would you choose these activities?

This exercise will help you think about what is really important, and reconnect with the purpose of the organization. Sometimes we get so caught up in trying to be everything at once that we forget what is essential. It's better to do two activities beautifully than six things half-heartedly.

Do Your Activities Fit Together?

Every layer of the strategy matters; they must all fit together like puzzle pieces. In trying to find areas needing improvement, ask yourself: do the activities fit well together?

A successful business ensures almost all aspects of their organization fit well with other parts, creating an efficient overall structure that aligns well with the organization's strategy and purpose.

For instance, in a musical band, every instrument must add to the rest, and reinforce the impact that the band wants to have on the audience. Any instrument or singer that does not synchronize well with the rest will be a source of disruption. The success factor does not depend on the number of different instruments that are playing, but on whether they work together to create harmony.

This is not to suggest that you must personally plan every detail, but that the individual in charge of deciding each factor should refer to the overall purpose to ensure that every activity, small or large, has a unifying frame. No major decision should be made without reference to purpose.

One weak activity can create discord within the entire system. Take a good look at your activities. Which of them provide the greatest value? Which ones do not?

Where Is Your Focus?

The critical question is not "How can I achieve?" but "What can I contribute?".

– Peter Drucker

Are you focusing on how you can get the most out of your customers (e.g. money), or on how you can offer them the most value and contribute to their lives?

Are you focusing on the needs of your customers? Your employees? Your community? All your stakeholders? Or only on the needs of your shareholders?

The answers to these questions can differentiate a good strategy from a great one, but watch out for other obstacles. Think about whether your company has any internal problems that might prevent you from taking these steps.

What part of your internal environment may not be supporting the strategy? What steps can you take to improve this situation? These are the kinds of questions the next two chapters will tackle. Although the topics they address are not always in the spotlight, those steps can make or break a company, and they are just as important as the other steps in the overall PDG Model.

THE PDG MODEL

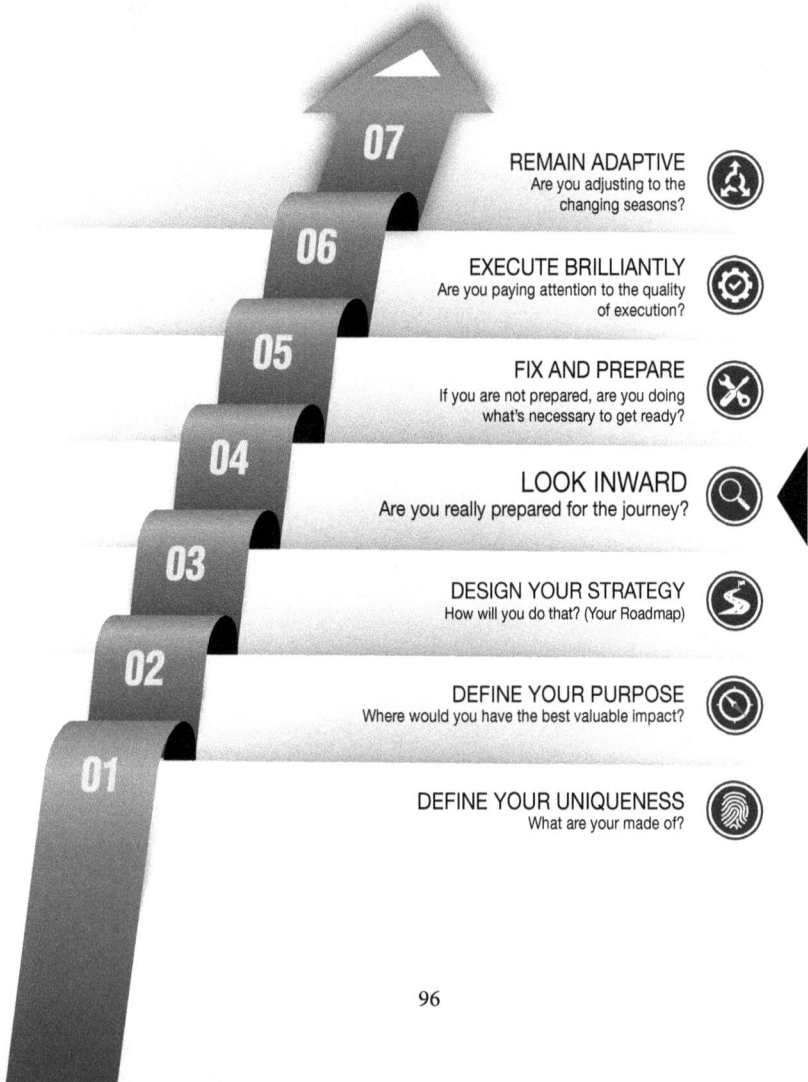

07 REMAIN ADAPTIVE
Are you adjusting to the changing seasons?

06 EXECUTE BRILLIANTLY
Are you paying attention to the quality of execution?

05 FIX AND PREPARE
If you are not prepared, are you doing what's necessary to get ready?

04 LOOK INWARD
Are you really prepared for the journey?

03 DESIGN YOUR STRATEGY
How will you do that? (Your Roadmap)

02 DEFINE YOUR PURPOSE
Where would you have the best valuable impact?

01 DEFINE YOUR UNIQUENESS
What are your made of?

CHAPTER FOUR

LOOK INWARD

> If you don't understand the details of your business you are going to fail
>
> *– Jeff Bezos*

Are you really prepared for the journey?

The **biggest** threat of failure comes not from the outside.

It comes from **within.**

Do you fully understand the internal workings of your organization? Awareness, or looking inward, is the fourth crucial step in the PDG Model. It is about assessing the actual foundation on which you want to build your strategy.

What prevents the strategy from coming to fruition? What parts of the organization stand in the way? What parts are an advantage?

Unless the internal workings of your organization run smoothly, your strategy is worth nothing more than words on a paper stored in the back of a dusty office, and it will not see the light of day.

Observing Your Organization

> To diagnose a system or yourself while in the midst of action requires the ability to achieve some distance from those on-the-ground events... to gain the distanced perspective you need to see what is really happening.
>
> – *Ronald A. Heifetz*

Looking inward means objectively analyzing your organization. A system is made up of many different working parts, with each one intricately connected to the next. In observing your organization, you cannot look at each separate part, but must look at how they come together as a whole.

This observation is different, almost opposite, from the way you looked at the company to discover its uniqueness. That analysis focused on your strengths and experiences; this analysis focuses on understanding **why** these are your strengths, what potential problems could obstruct them, and how your weaknesses affect them.

Ask yourself: what does the organization look like?

How does it function? To realize the organization's full potential, you need to be aware of every nook and cranny, every nut and bolt, and how they work together. To know whether your strategy will succeed, you need to understand the machine you are running, the people running it, and what bumps it may encounter on its journey.

Let us consider the two perspectives that are crucial to understanding an organization; the physical and the psychological.

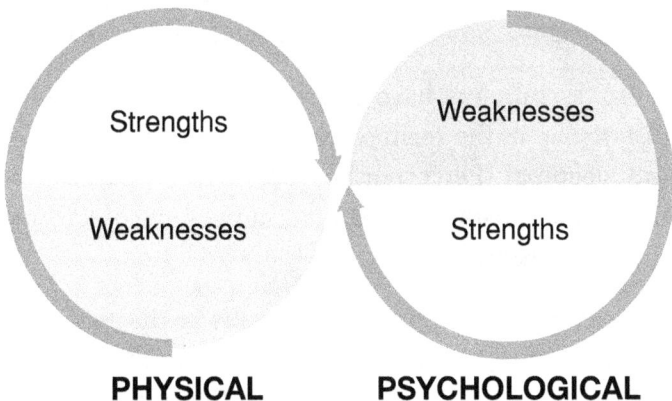

Figure 4.1:
General diagnostic model

Physical

The first perspective from which to observe your organization is the physical. The physical perspective includes everything tangible that the company needs, from money, assets, and resources to technology and staff. Physical problems are relatively easier to solve than psychological ones (if you have the money).

To solve physical problems, even if the solutions are simple, you first need to understand what's wrong. You need to be aware of the resources you have. Do you have enough people? Are your employees well-trained technically? Is your technology advanced enough? Are your processes streamlined and up-to-date? Do you have enough money to finance your activities and projects? Is the organizational structure functional? Do you have enough space, tools, equipment, and tangible assets?

Just as humans have bodies and require constant sustenance in the form of eating, drinking, breathing and sleeping, the corporate body of an organization also needs constant sustenance, in the form of various kinds of resources.

Being aware of physical problems is the first step toward solving them. Are you being honest with yourself about the amount of supplies or the employees you need? What resources should you invest more money into? What parts of your organization are weighing you down? What aspects cost you more than they benefit you?

Each of these questions must be answered accurately. Keep your diagnoses realistic. Know when and where you need to focus your attention, otherwise your strategy will be obstructed. If you don't have the means to deal with your problems, find other creative solutions – the issues must be tackled, not swept under the rug. Problems do not magically disappear.

Psychological

The second perspective from which to consider your organization is the psychological one. This includes the relationships of individuals within the organization, the mindsets and motivations of the employees and their authorities, and the values, priorities, beliefs, assumptions, and default behaviors that are part of the organization and its culture. It is extremely important, yet often underestimated.

>>

Culture eats strategy for breakfast.

– *Peter Drucker*

<<

When did you last take a step back to observe the behavioral dynamics your organization inspires? Sometimes we get so caught up in the day-to-day processes that we forget to consider what is happening around us. Culture is firmly cemented into the identity of your organization, and is slow and difficult to change.

>>

Culture is the deeper level of basic assumptions and beliefs that are shared by members of an organization, that operate unconsciously and define in a basic "taken for granted" fashion an organization's view of its self and its environment.

– Edgar Schein

«

Put simply, culture is the way things are naturally done in an organization

Culture is a very potent word, and it includes a wide range of values, mindsets, behaviors, rituals, traditions, and folk stories, each highly connected to the others.

In speaking of a culture's values, we must look at the values of three different levels – levels which I call the **3Ps: Purpose, Process, and Participation.**

- The first level focuses on the values embedded within the organization's purpose. What values does the purpose instill within the organization and its employees?

- The second level shifts to the process, which entails the strategies, policies, procedures, and the modus operandi – do they support the purpose or contradict it?

- The third level is the participation, or the actual behaviors on the ground. Do the employees follow the organizational values? Is there a gap between the values that are manifested in their behavior and the aspired organizational values?

For the organization to run smoothly, **Purpose, Process, and Participation should align**, and should each be moving forward. If this is not happening, work becomes arduous.

For example, if a restaurant's purpose is to provide healthy food and adhere to the highest standards of cleanliness, but the rules, policies, and actual operation do not follow the same standards, there will be problems. Similarly, if the restaurant does have rigorous hygiene rules, but the employees do not believe in these rules or share similar values of hygiene, they may neglect them. Additionally, if the management focuses on the speed of service and getting as many clients in as fast as possible, the focus on hygiene may take a back seat. In this case, what the restaurant projects doesn't match the behavior and beliefs in actual practice.

It is important for the values projected within the purpose to match the actual policies that are assigned and prioritized, and it is important that the employees believe in the values.

Understanding Your Values

»

Values are shaped and refined by rubbing against real problems, and people interpret their problems according to the values they hold.

– Ronald A. Heifetz

«

Values are not easy to change and are closely connected with behavior. Your values influence your decisions and actions, which become ingrained patterns that are difficult to change.

For example, imagine a company where employees are rewarded for achieving their targets, and are used to competing with their colleagues in an everyone-for-themselves mentality. Now imagine your new strategy requires a more cooperative environment, where credit and rewards are shared equally. The employees may find it challenging to adjust to this sudden shift. Further distrust and demotivation might arise.

»

Chains of habit are too light to be felt until they are too heavy to be broken.

– Warren Buffett

«

It is important that you understand your values and remain strictly committed to those that are related to your purpose, otherwise you risk being inauthentic and will lose credibility as an organization.

Based on Patrick Lencioni's book, *The Advantage,* an organization may have four types of values: core, aspirational, permission-to-play, and accidental.

Core values are inherent within the organization, will not change, and there are only two or three of them. An example of core values could be creating products or services that contribute to make people's lives better. Core values must be ones that differentiate you from other organizations.

Aspirational values are ones the organization aspires to have. For instance, collaboration may be a value that a company with a competitive atmosphere wants to adopt in the future.

Permission-to-play values are the minimum behavioral standards required – for instance, integrity and honesty. These are the bare minimum that all members of the organization must possess.

Lastly, ***accidental values*** are ones the organization has adopted, but which are not necessarily useful. This usually happens when employees' values become integrated into the values of the organization. These values do not pose a problem if they do not clash with the core values of the organization.

»

Culture does not change because we desire to change it. Culture changes when the organization is transformed; the culture reflects the realities of people working together every day.

– Frances Hesselbein

«

To properly understand the culture of an organization, you must understand the values – what the organization deems important and considers the correct way of behaving. How do you go about understanding these values? One method is to pay attention to the daily default behaviors.

Default behaviors are the natural and usual patterns we continuously follow, behaviors we have consistently adhered to for a long time. They are an important indicator of what each employee values and what the overall system encourages and motivates.

Analyzing Behaviors

»

Behavior is the mirror in which everyone shows their image.

– Johann Wolfgang Van Goethe

«

When you are considering these behaviors, pay special attention to the power dynamics. There is a difference between formal authority and power.

Which departments and which people hold the REAL power? You must be able to answer this question to properly understand the relationships within your organization. Think about how people respond to each other. It may be that an employee in the marketing department is considered crucial to your company's success, and therefore holds the respect and admiration of their colleagues. It could be that the sales department controls the strategy of the others.

The role of power is extremely important, because people will change their behavior according to who has the power or who has the most say. You will need to assess who has the power to make decisions.

In each department, who is in charge of implementing the strategy? Is s/he suffering from any form of power struggle? If so, what changes will smooth out the flow of power?

Those with formal titles might not hold the greatest amount of power – sometimes it's the individuals behind the scenes. **People respond more to power than titles;** by observing behavior, you can tell where the true power lies.

Another way to assess default behaviors is to examine how the organization deals with conflict.

1. When a problem arises, do individuals hide behind others, avoiding accountability?

2. Are tasks clearly assigned to each individual, and do those individuals take full responsibility for their tasks?

3. How often does the organization take risks?

4. How is innovation rewarded, or failure punished?

There are other options for understanding an organization. Consider the rituals and traditions the organization takes part in. For example, when it is someone's birthday, if the whole office celebrates and gets a cake, that shows a great deal about the office dynamics, especially when compared with a company where nobody celebrates because the relationship between the staff is not intimate enough.

Traditions and rituals reflect the office dynamics and how people work together. No single way of implementing these traditions or rituals is correct; you have to consider how well they fit with the purpose and strategy. Do they hinder or help your purpose? The point of behavioral habits is to create the right environment and to get everyone on the same page, moving in unison so as not to create dissonance.

Creating The Right Environment

》

What makes adaptation complicated is that it involves deciding what is so essential that it must be preserved going forward and what of all that you value can be left behind.

– Ronald A. Heifetz

《

The major objective of looking inward is to analyze the entire system, assessing which elements function well and thrive, and which do not. Look at each separate entity, tradition, or activity, and inquire whether it aids the implementation of the strategy and purpose of the organization.

If the answer is "yes", then the activity is crucial, and it is essential to reinforce this type of behavior so that it continues.

If the answer is "no", however, your next step is more complicated; you will have to choose whether to alter, fix, or completely discard this element.

To clarify the above processes, pretend you are an outsider coming to work in your organization for the first time.

1. As a new employee, how quickly can you discern the organization's purpose?

2. Do the tasks, rituals, and traditions clearly reflect the declared identity of the organization?

3. Are the rituals and traditions shared by the entire system? What are they?

4. As an outsider, what is your first impression of the organization? What is the organization's reputation in the market? Do they match?

5. What stories do the employees tell? What do the customers say about it?

6. Does the work environment in the company inspire and motivate individuals to implement the strategy? How?

7. How often are people engaged in major structural changes?

8. How's the morale? Is there a shortage of energy buzz?

9. How often does the organization call for a new strategy? How often does it ask for direction?

10. How does it diagnose the problems it encounters when implementing its strategies?

> Outsiders have the intuitive ability to continually view problems in fresh ways and to identify ineffective practices and traditions.
>
> – *John P. Kotter*

For companies to move forward, they need a clear system of accountability and trust, otherwise employees may hide problems or try to blame others. Such behavior will only hinder growth. **The environment must motivate honesty, transparency, and courage**, so that individuals are not afraid to state the truth.

In environments that inspire trust and teamwork, employees feel more comfortable and willing to address problems at hand. When the environment is strict, it becomes frightening to make a mistake. Employees may resort to blaming others and avoiding responsibility. This behavior can cause major problems for an organization.

If the environment isn't open enough for employees to address problems freely, many issues could arise without higher management even hearing about them – at least until it is too late. Real progress will be hindered by cover-ups and people trying to avoid blame, and this behavior will create obstacles when it comes to implementing the strategy.

For example, when Samsung released the Note 7 phone, there was a problem with the battery that made it dangerous and, in some instances, it literally burst into flames. At this point you begin to wonder which employees knew this was a problem and why none of them spoke up.

You must have a balance. You want an open environment where your staff do not fear being penalized just because problems occur. At the same time, work is work, deadlines need to be met, and productivity is a must. Too much leniency can slow down productivity, but too little leniency may instill a culture of fear, as no one wants to face the repercussions of making a mistake.

You need to know:

1. Are your staff motivated?

2. Are they able to do their work?

3. Is what motivates them aligned with the purpose?

4. Do they share the goals and beliefs of the organization?

5. Are their values aligned with yours? If not, they could be moving in a different direction, resulting in more obstacles and friction.

6. What are their abilities?

7. Do they have the skills necessary to carry out the strategy?

8. Are they involved in the drawing up of the strategy?

9. Do they coordinate with others to achieve shared and common goals?

10. Do others help them fulfill their responsibilities, or do they undermine them?

11. Do they have the tools they need?

12. Does the physical environment support them or act as a barrier?

13. Are they drowning in an overflow of data?

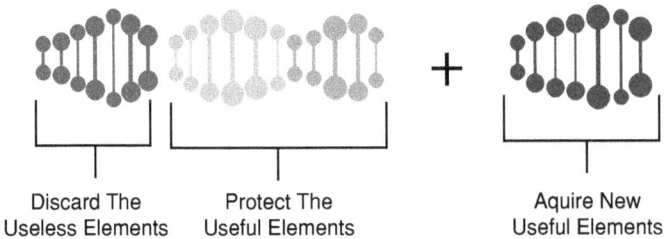

| Discard The Useless Elements | Protect The Useful Elements | Aquire New Useful Elements |

Figure 4.2:
Adaptive behavior

The roots of a company's culture run deep, so it will take time to pull out those roots and replant the culture. There are always points of weakness in any company, and they should be expected. There is no need to panic, but it is important for you to be aware of the problems and start ironing out the bumps, so the strategy can have its best chance at success. If you have ever tried to solve a psychological problem, you know just how hard it can be. You must isolate the behaviors that started the pattern, and change them. The process of change can be grueling, but you must start somewhere.

What Does Your Culture Enforce?

What values does your culture encourage?

Just as a leader requires strong values to push forward and succeed, so do cultures. Values such as integrity and professionalism should be at the core of a good organization's culture. Furthermore, it is not enough just to declare these values; they must be applied.

Values do not really exist unless they are part of day-to-day interactions. They must be built into the DNA of the organization and demonstrated by everyone. Nobody should be exempt or excused from following the core values, or the entire system may crumble. Those in charge *especially* should embody these characteristics, because they set an example for the rest of the staff.

With leadership and a clear purpose and strategy, the employees will understand the importance of the organizational values and will be able to incorporate them into their personal value systems. This will offer them a clear framework to work from, defining their roles in line with the organization's values. In turn, the strategy will become easier to implement. Employees will almost instinctively know what actions go against the values, and the different parts of the system will work in unison as they uphold the values and fulfill the organization's purpose.

If some employees are unmotivated or do not share similar values, problems will arise not only for them, but for the entire system. If a few people go against the values, the others will become confused. Trust is essential for a healthy work environment, so everyone must be on the same page for the culture to be effective.

Do You Have What It Takes?

Strategy is made up of the choices you must make and the steps you must take to fulfill a certain purpose. The moment you create a strategy, you will have made a decision to change a part of your current reality. However, there are other questions to be answered. For instance:

Possible Obstacles

1. Are there barriers to making that change? What are they?

2. What are the challenges you will face when implementing your strategy? How are you planning to overcome them?

3. What realities are you currently ignoring? What are you avoiding? What assumptions are you relying on? What potential problems are you discounting?

4. Do you have access to the necessary resources? Have you secured enough for your implementation?

5. Is your strategy clear and easily communicated? Is your plan realistic? Are your priorities achievable?

6. Is everyone capable and properly motivated?

7. Do people know what data is required for critical decisions, and how to make that information available in a systematic way?

Culture

1. Will your organizational culture allow you to take the necessary steps to implement your strategy, or will it stand in the way?

2. Does the organization's culture have what it takes to bridge the gap between where you are and where you want to go? If not, what could you do to adapt and change the mindsets of those around you?

3. Does the culture encourage knowledge-sharing and communication?

4. Is the culture adaptive enough? Resilient enough?

5. What aspects of the culture should be preserved and cherished? Which ones should be discarded?

6. What new enabling aspects should be acquired?

7. Does everyone take full responsibility for their successes and failures? How can your organization ensure that people are held responsible?

8. What is the level of friction among key stakeholders? Who can work with whom? Who are the parties that are tightly involved in decision-making, but cannot work together? How can this friction be minimized?

9. Are there cliques of power within the organization?

10. Does the authority system project harmony? Or does it project internal power struggles?

Roles

1. Is everyone aligned with the strategy and the purpose? If not, why?

2.   Are roles clearly defined? If not, what does your organization need to do to define them?

3.   Who will be involved in the creation, implementation, and execution of the strategy? Are they skilled and qualified? Are they empowered and authorized?

4.   Do the people in key roles have the information they need to make their decisions?

Organizational Structure

1.   Does your organization's structure (hierarchy, roles, standards, norms, rules, etc.) help the implementation of your strategy?

2.   Are the standards, regulations, and procedures in line with your organization's purpose?

3.   How flexible and adaptive are the processes and procedures?

Proper systems safeguarding transparency and accountability will allow less room for vacillation, and more room for the unified perspective and cooperative environment you seek to achieve.

This cooperative environment shows why purpose is so important in the PDG Model. With purpose, the focus falls not on making the biggest deals or the most money, but on helping the greatest number of people in a profitable manner. Ideally this would mean that, if you did not know how to do something, or felt someone else could do it better, you would not hesitate to ask for help. This would not be a sign of weakness; it would be a part of the job, in line with the greater purpose of making sure that the stakeholders are taken care of. If care for the stakeholders became everyone's focus and was drilled into the actions of the employees, there would be less room for straying and more room for teamwork.

Whole Foods Market is a prime example of a company that focuses on purpose and uses it to guide its decisions. In the book, *Conscious Capitalism*, John Mackey and Raj Sisodia show how Whole Foods makes sure that the individuals and stakeholders within the organization are satisfied, which exemplifies how focusing on purpose can translate into success.

In one Whole Foods store in West Hartford, Connecticut, the cash registers stopped working during a snowstorm. The lines of customers waiting to pay grew long, and the customers in line became increasingly stressed as they watched the storm worsen and worried about the drive home. The assistant team leader running the store that day made a quick decision with his other team members. They decided that until they could fix the registers (which took about thirty minutes) they would let the customers take their groceries without paying. They lost about $4,000 worth of groceries, but received something worth far more. One of the clients, overwhelmed by this generosity and kindness, wrote a letter praising the act and how she felt it embodied the Christmas spirit. This letter ended up in the media (and eventually in books), resulting in publicity worth far more than $4,000.

The intention, however, was not to gain publicity. The team at the store did what they thought was right, showing they cared about their customers and would put the customers' concerns above their own need to make money. Ideal organizations focus on strengthening the relationships between the various stakeholders. When everyone is happy, this produces a beautiful and rewarding relationship.

The First Steps Of Change

If you keep trying to solve a deadlocked problem the same way, it will not be fixed

This sounds simple enough, but unfortunately not everyone thinks it through.

Do you want to implement significant changes in the culture? There are no magic fixes, no wonderful instant solutions. Change is tough and sometimes you will want to turn back, but when executed properly, looking inward can work miracles for your business.

You can even think about looking inward on a personal level. You may have planned out the amazing life down to the last detail, but if you do not believe in yourself, or you haven't dealt with certain personal problems that hold you back (e.g. fear of commitment, fear of the unknown, fear of failing), will it be possible to follow through?

By looking inward, you recognize the obstacles that keep your organization (or you) from implementing your strategy. This requires understanding the relationships and group dynamics that affect all decisions, and pinpointing where something needs to change. Looking inward is about understanding the values and beliefs driving the non-functional behaviors you want to change.

Awareness requires looking inward. It takes time and if it is not done carefully and confidently, it will not succeed.

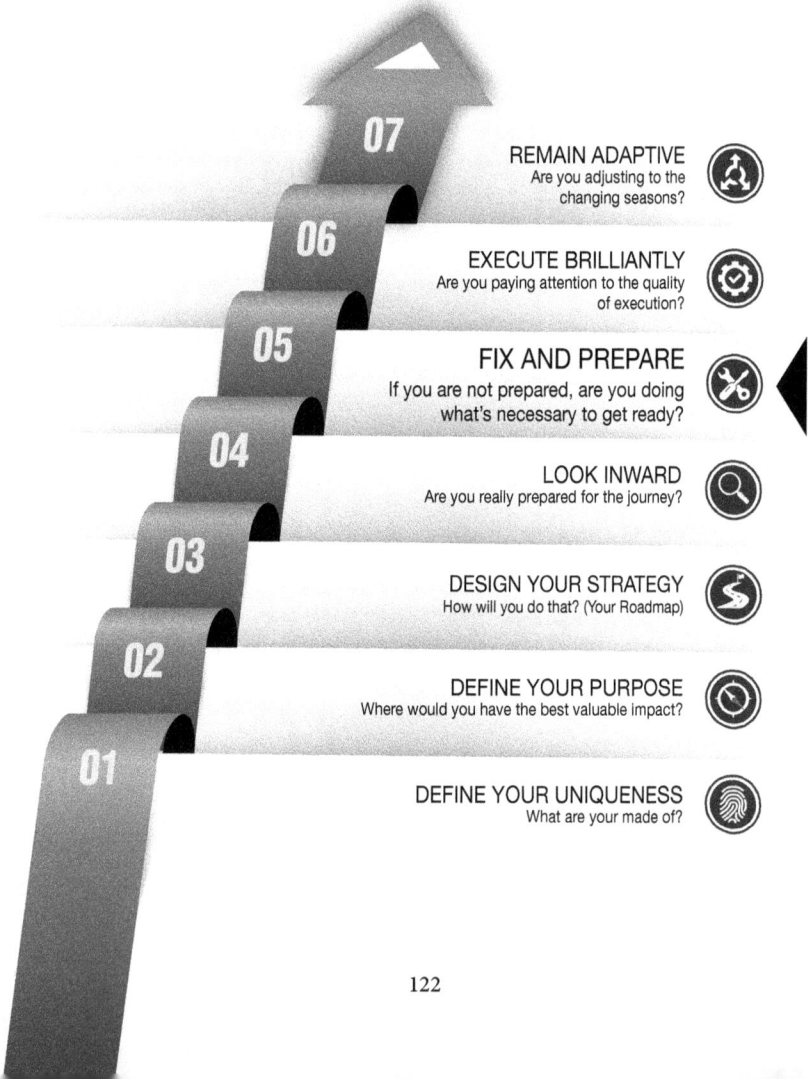

THE PDG MODEL

07

REMAIN ADAPTIVE
Are you adjusting to the changing seasons?

06

EXECUTE BRILLIANTLY
Are you paying attention to the quality of execution?

05

FIX AND PREPARE
If you are not prepared, are you doing what's necessary to get ready?

04

LOOK INWARD
Are you really prepared for the journey?

03

DESIGN YOUR STRATEGY
How will you do that? (Your Roadmap)

02

DEFINE YOUR PURPOSE
Where would you have the best valuable impact?

01

DEFINE YOUR UNIQUENESS
What are your made of?

122

CHAPTER FIVE

FIX AND PREPARE

> » The relevant question is not simply what shall we do tomorrow, but rather what shall we do today in order to get ready for tomorrow.
>
> *– Peter Drucker*

Are you ready to execute your strategy? Have you removed the obstacles or barriers standing in the way of your strategy?

Although it is a critical first step, acknowledging that problems exist falls short of giving you solutions to fixing them. The "fix and prepare" step takes the information about barriers which you learned from the "look inward step", and actually addresses those barriers.

Over the years, I have sat on the boards of several organizations, and I have also advised many others. A classical scenario that I often witness is organizations contracting large consulting firms to help them define their uniqueness, articulate their purpose, and design the right strategies, at exorbitant costs. However, the organization then remains stuck in mediocrity, or fails to successfully apply the strategy. Unfortunately, it is not unusual for the offices of CEOs to contain thick binders of fancy, multi-million dollar strategy documents that are collecting dust. Years after consultants have spent months designing brilliant strategies, little, if any, progress has been made.

Why is that the case? Change can be hard. It is often accompanied with loss, pain, and resistance. The whole process of trying to fix it can be scary. It can be tough. There are moments when you may question whether introducing change was necessary or wise. If you begin to doubt yourself, don't worry. That might be an indication that you are on the right track.

Fixing a system often requires a change in perspective. If your organization is stuck and can't take advantage of the purpose and strategy you have identified, however clear they may be, then perspectives, attitudes, and habits must be changed, or the system will only have brief moments of relief and success at best. This is the step where true leadership comes into play.

Leadership is in essence about mobilizing people to fix their dysfunctional thinking and behavior, and preparing them to capture opportunities for progress. Exercising leadership may require creating purposeful discomfort in order to implement the desired change when necessary – to get the system unstuck and moving forward. The earlier anecdote is a testament to how often organizations fail to implement strategies because they hesitate, or fail, to exercise leadership and mobilize individuals to overcome the barriers and build on their capacities – which is necessary for the implementation of the strategy, the fulfillment of the purpose, and the organization's continued survival and growth.

Without this step, strategy, purpose, and even survival and growth could be at risk. Ignoring or mishandling this step can cause even the largest organizations, with the smartest strategies and most abundant resources, to fail to progress.

The "fix and prepare" step is probably the hardest in the PDG Model. You are likely to encounter resistance, pain, and possibly even casualties. It cannot be rushed; it will take time, thought, and effort. Do not be discouraged if you do not see instant results. Remember that when you introduce change in a system, you must keep an eye on the system's reactions to the change.

That being said, even after overcoming the obstacles standing in your way, your organization may need some time to stabilize and recover from the aftermath of your intervention. For example, imagine that you have shut down a department that is losing money, and reallocated its staff to other divisions. This intervention may have stopped your organization's financial bleeding, solving the problem. However, it may still take months for your staff to productively integrate into the new divisions of the organization, and to get used to the adjustments.

Each case may be different, but this chapter will give you an overview of insights you might use when you exercise leadership and undergo this crucial step.

What Problems Are You Dealing With?

>>

While technical problems may be very complex and critically important... they have known solutions that can be implemented by current know-how ... Adaptive challenges can only be addressed through changes in people's priorities, beliefs, habits, and loyalties ... shedding certain entrenched ways, tolerating losses, and generating the new capacity to thrive anew.

– Ronald A. Heifetz

«

As we saw in the previous chapter, an organization can face two types of problems: the physical and the psychological.

However, the physical and psychological are often intertwined, which makes solving problems more complex. For example, suppose you need to change offices because the current one is too costly. Changing offices is not just a physical problem: it can also be considered a psychological one. Each employee will have to adjust to the new office. Perhaps it's a longer drive from home. This may seem to be a small adjustment, but it is not if an employee must pick up their children after work and the added commuting time alters their whole schedule.

It may not be practical to consider every possible effect a change may have on every single person, especially in a large organization. However, this example demonstrates why there will often be resistance when undergoing significant change, regardless of the popularity of the change or the person leading it.

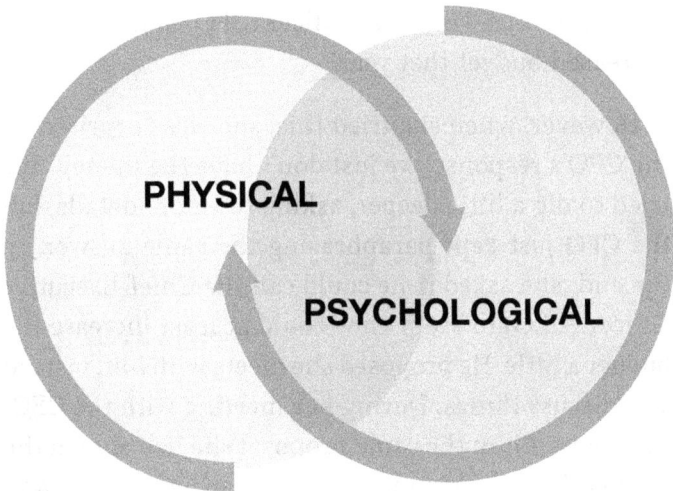

Figure 5.1:
The common nature of organizational challenges

I know a vice president of human resources, who told me a story that highlights the point I am trying to make. To keep the organization up to date, she would organize yearly training courses and workshops for the organization's employees. One year, as she was putting her affairs in order, she realized that the training budget was insufficient. It was an issue with a straightforward solution: increase the budget. The organization had brought in generous profits the previous year, so there was no shortage of funding. All she had to do was go to the Chief Financial Officer (CFO) and ask for an increased budget that year.

However, when she tried this, she was surprised by the CFO's response: we just don't have the money. She tried to dig a little deeper, asking for more details, but the CFO just kept paraphrasing the same answer. In the end, she asked if he could call the Chief Executive Officer (CEO) to see if they could at least increase the budget a little. He proposed she meets with him instead and discuss things. During her meeting with the CEO, she showed him the same proposal she had shown the CFO earlier. She summarized her earlier meeting and asked if it was possible to increase the budget. The CEO simply provided the same answer she heard over and over from the CFO. She confronted him, "how can there be no money? You sent us an email telling us that we met last year's target and more."

"To be honest, let's say I approve your proposal. We invest in the employees and then they end up leaving, which is what happened last year and the year before that."

Finally, the real issue surfaced. The CEO was hesitant to invest the organization's money in training the employees, only to have them leave and take their new acquired skills elsewhere. However, she did not let it go, but asked, "What if we don't train them and they stay?"

She struck a chord. The CEO paused, as if to think through the consequences of having loyal, but unqualified employees. They would not be able to do their jobs effectively, and this would actually end up hurting the organization's chances of sustaining its success. He changed his mind and approved the allocation of the additional training budget. The real reason behind the seemingly physical issue (lack of funding), was actually a psychological one – the CEO's concern over some employees using their enhanced qualifications to find jobs elsewhere.

It is important that when confronted with challenges, you ask yourself whether the nature of the challenge is physical or psychological. In the case of a physical challenge, try to go deeper and check if there might be a hidden psychological issue. When you are dealing with people, a physical issue often has a psychological element to it. Physical and psychological problems are at times interconnected, and they are both important to attend to.

Dealing With Change

> »
>
> Business and human endeavors are systems...we tend to focus on snapshots of isolated parts of the system. And wonder why our deepest problems never get solved.
>
> *– Peter Senge*
>
> «

Before implementing change, you must remember that your organization is a system and needs to be treated as such.

You need to remember how highly connected everything is. Each part acts interdependently, so a change in one part affects the rest of the system. You must also bear in mind that the system has enduring patterns of behavior. Breaking or fixing any of these patterns will be met with resistance.

These patterns exist because they benefit – sometimes in obscure ways – parts of the system. If you start interfering with the patterns, the beneficiaries will react, and because the system is interconnected, you will eventually see a reaction in other parts.

Sometimes upper management makes the mistake of thinking that what happens in one department will not affect the others, but think of a human body: if one organ is failing, other organs will eventually suffer and the survival of the entire body might be under threat.

For your organization to survive and grow, you must understand that proper change can only happen when most of its parts are aligned with it. Besides the individual identities of each person, the group (system) possesses an identity of its own. You must consider how you can mobilize individuals as well as groups – the change must address both the individual and the system. **Until most parts of the system are mobilized for change, no real change in group identity can happen.** Mobilization of the system is key.

A system is mainly concerned with guarding its own interests. Change must be framed in a way that furthers a system's interests. Instigating change creates uncertainty, discomfort, losses, and pain. This scares the system. If you don't communicate change in a way that highlights the benefits to the system, chaos and confusion can result. This makes having a clear and communicated purpose and strategy vital.

During my time at Reuters, a new CEO came in and tried to change and restructure the entire system. The company informed all those in senior-to-top management positions that nobody's job was secure anymore; all would be under review pending the final new structure. Meanwhile, a consulting company was hired to examine and recommend new structures for all the company's branches worldwide. The process lasted about two years, and during this time, the system was in a state of uncertainty, fear, and confusion.

Employees were hesitant about making major decisions, and most of their efforts were focused on retaining their jobs and securing their futures – they were playing it safe. The employees were in survival mode, and the atmosphere became tense and stressful, far from the upbeat, creative, and productive atmosphere everyone was used to. The organization came to a standstill – almost frozen – and progress stopped.

As after a late winter, growth took months to establish itself once the new structure was implemented. Unfortunately, the structure that took so long to realize – the one that created the standstill – did not last very long, and the company reverted to its previous model. It was not appropriate to the global nature of the company's operations and so did not work as well as the CEO had intended.

Introducing change is a difficult process that must carefully take into account the organization's purpose, culture, intended strategy, and the current and aspired realities. If it doesn't, the resulting chaos could push an organization into a rut it might not be able to get out of.

>>

In the midst of chaos, there is also opportunity.

– Sun Tzu

<<

The fix and prepare stage is challenging because you are attempting to alter parts of a system that are working against your aspirations and trying to prevent you from accomplishing this feat. If you do not find the right balance between stability and instability, this stage could have costly side effects.

Before you rock the boat, make sure it is necessary, and make sure you don't sink the boat in the process.

Tension Is Inevitable

People don't resist change. They resist being changed.

– Peter Senge

Tension almost always accompanies change. Remember that it is not the change itself that people fear; it is the pain that accompanies it. In fact, our drive for growth calls for beneficial change, and most people welcome and even strive for changes that they believe will benefit them (e.g. getting a promotion). It is the painful loss that accompanies some changes that makes people hesitant or resistant.

Tension lasts only until everyone involved has adjusted to the new process. Finding a balance between conflict and comfort means having just enough tension to spur change into action and achieve the desired difference, but not so much tension that people leave the organization.

>>

Your goal should be to keep the temperature within what we call the productive zone of disequilibrium (PZD): enough heat generated by your intervention to gain attention, engagement, and forward motion, but not so much that the organization (or your part of it) explodes.

– *Ronald A. Heifetz*

<<

When the heat gets turned up, resistance increases. Anyone exercising leadership must be aware of this effect. When facing a change, even a positive one, some employees and even authority figures may resist, trying to get things back to the familiar, the status quo, because it makes them comfortable and serves their own agendas. This resistance is counterproductive and must be dealt with.

For example, in a secretive culture prone to blaming others, the people who will most fiercely resist a change to an open and communicative environment are those who avoid taking responsibility for their actions. On the other hand, the ones who continually fall victim to undue blame will benefit from the change and so will encourage it.

To be able to mobilize people to embrace change, you will need to understand people's reactions. Tension is inevitable, but it can be dealt with. What you need to do is to help people navigate through the tension to bring about a new reality.

What Can You Do To Change?

One of the most common ways to overcome resistance to change is to educate people about it beforehand. Communication of ideas helps people see the need for and the logic of a change.

– John P. Kotter

Now that we know change makes systems uncomfortable, let's discuss some of the many ways that an organization can chart a successful course through purposeful change.

One way is by improving communications within the company; this is actually one of the fundamental tools to changing mindsets. People need to feel that their views are important and that their thoughts will be acted upon. If people feel they can talk freely about their issues, and their complaints will result in fair and reasonable resolutions, you have the basis for a healthy environment. You don't want people to feel uncomfortable or hold back because they fear being berated for their views.

»

> A hallmark of a healthy creative culture is that its people feel free to share ideas, opinions, and criticisms. Lack of candour, if unchecked, ultimately leads to dysfunctional environments.
>
> *– Ed Catmull*

«

Additionally, the organization must communicate honestly the trade-offs and risks associated with the planned change. If people are not prepared for these, they may become discouraged, and may also grow distrustful because they won't feel the organization trusts them with relevant information. This will lead to a lack of communication on both sides, so ensure the implications of change – positive and negative – are presented clearly and openly.

Gathering support and mobilizing people is also essential for change. One of the effective forms of support is mobilizing informal authority, which can be a powerful tool when approaching a significant challenge. Informal authority refers to anyone who holds sway over the organization, but does not have the title to match their importance. They are opinion leaders who others look to for direction.

As well as informal authority, you need to strengthen the other relationships you have, and build up your credibility within the system. Try to support as many initiatives as you can (without disrupting your purpose), in order to garner support when you yourself need to implement changes.

Leak tidbits of your plan to gauge reactions. Where will your colleagues stand on the spectrum of resistance? Who are your supporters? Who are your opponents? When the problem you are trying to fix relates to the culture or is psychological by nature, you will need as many supporters as possible.

Listen to as many people as you can; you will understand different perspectives on the problem and the proposed solutions. You may then be able to find compromises which allow your plan to move forward with minimal resistance.

If there isn't resistance, deep change is probably not happening

It takes time to change mentalities. You do not want to push people so hard that they become resentful and angry. At the same time, there should be some pressure for change, or nothing will happen. There will be losses at times, but these should not discourage you, your organization, or its stakeholders.

If your organization can undergo the productive tension and resistance that follows the introduction of a psychological change, the experience will strengthen its resilience, and prepare it for future changes.

Lastly, make sure you are clear about what your role

is in the change initiative. How are you facilitating it? Are you leading the change? Do you hold a position of authority that can help make the transition smoother?

It is also important to consider what roles the other stakeholders play in the change initiative. Keeping in mind that everyone involved will impact upon the change, hindering or helping it depending on where they stand.

Who Is On Your Side During The Change?

Form alliances and build up your army of supporters, partners, and allies, because if things go south, you do not want to be on the battlefield alone.

It is important to be familiar with the individuals who might resist the change. The more you get to know them and spend time with them, the more you can soften the impact the change will have on them. You will also be able to tell how much resistance you are likely to face, so you will be able to properly prepare and ensure your plans come to fruition.

People shift their alliances. One day they will be telling you they will support you through thick and thin; the next day, the opposition may have offered them a sweeter deal and they will be batting for the other team. This can tell you a lot about your progress. It will be frustrating, but if you stick to your purpose, keep an adaptive strategy, and move past the discomfort, your efforts will be worthwhile.

Different groups also need different forms of persuasion to be convinced about changes. Some people respond to hard proof and logical reasoning, while others require you to target their hearts rather than their minds. Know your audience and anticipate their needs, because understanding your constituents is a fundamental requirement to garner support.

Furthermore, although they will most likely be against you, the skeptics in the company can be your most valuable assets. The skeptic is thorough, actively working to find faults in your plan, and they will not shy away from telling you exactly what is wrong with it. Listening to varying opinions can help you clarify the overall picture. Instead of discounting what the skeptic says, use it to fortify your argument and identify weaknesses that you can address. Once you have pacified the skeptic, you know you have secured a winning plan for change.

Will You Need Surgery?

The most common leadership failure stems from trying to apply technical solutions to adaptive challenges.

– *Ronald A. Heifetz*

One of the biggest mistakes many organizations will make is trying to solve a psychological issue with a physical solution.

Physical solutions are similar to bandaging or stitching a wound. For a small or superficial cut, a bandage is sufficient. If the cut goes a little deeper, stitches will be necessary. However, the problem arises when the wound requires surgery. You must cut deeply to fix the problem, and the risks escalate – moving into the realm of psychological issues.

Psychological problems require various interventions at multiple levels. Once you define a problem as psychological, it is no longer up to the authority alone to resolve the issue. Solving the problem requires collaborative effort. The only path to success involves contributions from all the people concerned.

Imagine a psychological problem involving a change in the code of conduct: no matter how logical the change is and how many times authority communicates it, if the employees do not see the benefit behind this change, they will be unconvinced and find it difficult to adopt the new rules. The employees standing on the opposing side of change may decrease the chance for these new rules to become part of the organization.

Psychological problems can be daunting because they require rebuilding beliefs and patterns of behavior over the entire system – changing people's mindsets. A psychologist may need months to help one person change habits and behaviors – now multiply that up enough to apply it to an organization with hundreds, or even thousands, of individuals.

Before we proceed to the next part, note that not every situation requires psychological changes. If the organization functions well, if it is fulfilling its purpose, and if you can honestly say your stakeholders are happy and satisfied, then continue doing what you are doing – but keep an eye on potential issues so you can respond quickly if they deteriorate in the future.

Have We Accurately Diagnosed The Challenges?

Before attempting to solve a problem, you must make sure you have identified it correctly. Remember, you cannot treat an infected wound with painkillers. The latter will only alleviate the pain temporarily while you work to clean the wound and prescribe the appropriate antibiotics. You must know whether your organization is dealing with a physical or psychological issue.

If you find that it is facing a psychological issue, you will need to check if the members of the system understand the nature of the problem and how urgent and significant it is to resolve it.

One way to do that is to gauge your employees' understanding of the problem. When asked to explain the issue, how do your employees respond? Do they really know the problem? Do they give you a straightforward answer, or do they give you long answers that try to shift your attention away from the subject? Are they telling you stories or exaggerating what the problem may be? Are they blaming others for what may be their own fault? Are they trying to run away from the problem instead of facing it?

You must make sure that everyone concerned recognizes the issue. Make sure employees understand how detrimental the problem could be. Once they understand the gravity of the issue, they can take the necessary steps to learn about it and collaborate to fix it.

Remember to keep competing priorities in mind. The parties involved see the problem from their own angles, looking at how it benefits them, or doesn't. People have their own commitments and loyalties that encourage them to push for different outcomes. **It is important that you understand people's perspectives on the problem,** otherwise you will face resistance that can make it difficult for you to resolve the problem fully.

Although we would like to think there are always win-win situations, most of the time there aren't. There are trade-offs, and unfortunately you rarely get exactly what you want.

»

The challenge of leadership when trying to generate adaptive change is to work with differences, passions, and conflicts in a way that diminishes their destructive potential and constructively harnesses their energy.

– Ronald A. Heifetz

«

When companies try to present win-win solutions, sometimes they fail to look deeply enough into the system. They may avoid making necessary sacrifices because they want to stave off painful decisions.

For example, a company that wants to market a new product also wants to keep down the costs. If the marketing department needs $1,000,000 to create an impactful campaign but the board is unwilling to make that investment, they have different priorities. The board may only give the marketing department $100,000, which makes it hard for them to implement the campaign effectively. In the end, it becomes a lose-lose situation if nobody buys the product because the marketing campaign was an utter failure, and the $100,000 was wasted.

Think Before You (Re)Act

»

Knowing how the environment is pulling your strings and playing you is critical to making responsive rather than reactive moves.

– *Ronald A. Heifetz*

«

One of our downfalls is making reactive decisions. How often have you seen someone make a decision based on spur-of-the-moment emotions? We need to step back and see the bigger picture, examining our purpose and the options ahead of us before making a decision. Reacting emotionally can be blinding, resulting in decisions that may negatively affect us.

For example, imagine that the top bank in the country decided to introduce a new ATM equipped with an artificially intelligent virtual assistant. However, after installing the prototype in a few locations, they discovered that the virtual assistant was underdeveloped and did not function correctly. The bank decided to scrap the project and cut their losses. Meanwhile, a competing bank, unaware of the problems with this new ATM, reacted impulsively. It did not wait to see if the ATM would be functional or accepted by the public, but immediately began drawing up plans for a similar device. Because they rushed to follow their competitor, instead of waiting to see if the project worked or looking for their own innovations, they also wasted time and resources that might have been used elsewhere.

This example illustrates our visceral instincts, our first reactions when we face promising opportunities or emotional issues. When we react, our consideration for the action is only short-term and lacks purpose.

At the other end of the spectrum is the mind that calculates before acting. When individuals act responsively rather than reactively, they respond in a way that they feel is in line with their purpose, rather than a way that gratifies their anger. This distinction is extremely important; it can be the difference between right and wrong decisions.

Are the decisions of your organization, boss, or stakeholders often reactive or responsive? Many organizations and bosses make rash decisions under pressure because they respond emotionally rather than rationally.

Organizations become reactive when they want to solve problems immediately and do not take the time to fully consider their options. They may try to raise employees' salaries instead of their morale. They may decide that buying new computers will help the staff work faster. They refuse to dig deeper to find the real issues, and instead they throw money at the problem, hoping it will resolve itself.

When your organization encounters a problem, don't let your instincts take control. Our desire for quick-fixes and instant solutions is strong, but if you try to solve something deep with a superficial patch, the problem will bubble back to the surface again, possibly in a worse form. Clean out the whole wound; tackle the problem at its root before it gets worse.

The Role Of Authority

Before changes can take place, you need to make sure authority is on board.

According to Heifetz, authority refers to anyone "entrusted with power in return for services". This could be workplace management, bosses, teachers, parents, or the government. You do not need to be in a position of authority to exercise leadership, although it can make exercising leadership easier, and the best types of authority do exercise leadership, mobilizing people to change for the better.

It is vital to keep authority informed. The authority figure should know the potential risks of the changes you hope to implement. If things go south, you want the support of authority, and you may not have this if you have withheld information or they are unprepared for the issues.

At times, authority will make the mistake of taking on too much responsibility. For the organization to run smoothly, tasks should be shared and their weight spread across employees. If authority keeps taking too much of the responsibility and is therefore unable to perform its normal tasks, the entire organization suffers. By sharing the burden, the pressure does not fall solely on one individual. If you are the authority figure, your biggest strengths may become weaknesses if everyone relies upon you. True leadership makes employees both independent and interdependent.

It is important to understand that authority figures are not responsible for fixing every problem. However, they do make some of the harder decisions, and resolving competing commitments often falls into this category. Authority figures may create tension by favoring one option over the other, and you must understand that what some might consider an unfair decision may sometimes be necessary. Compromises often cause more issues than they solve, and can be detrimental to the entire system. While difficult, picking sides often is exactly what is necessary, and can even be one form of exercising leadership.

Growth And Learning

>>

They [leaders] motivate and inspire others to go in the right direction and they, along with everyone else, sacrifice to get there.

– John P. Kotter

<<

Real change can only be implemented by true leadership. True leadership occurs when people are pushed out of their comfort zone to grow and become stronger, like baby birds being pushed out of the nest to learn to fly.

The person who does not go beyond placing a toe in to test the water will miss out on all the gifts of the ocean

Now I would like you to think back to times when you exercised leadership, creating the type of atmosphere that mobilized your organization. What types of behavior were you rewarding? Did you keep your employees in their comfort zones, or did you intentionally place them in challenging situations, making them grow as individuals? Offering employees a chance to grow is not about filling job positions, but about nurturing people who will flourish along with the organization. The more capabilities your employees acquire, and the more opportunities they have to learn and grow, the more valuable they will be in your organization.

The type of environment you harness can affect whether employees feel inspired and encouraged enough to experiment, learn, and grow. The most successful companies did not succeed by sticking to the status quo; rather, they took risks. Of course, not all risks lead to progress and growth, but your organization can only truly prosper if it takes intelligent risks. As Abraham Maslow states,

"One can choose to go back toward safety or forward toward growth. Growth must be chosen again and again; fear must be overcome again and again."

People exercising leadership are meant to pass the torch and mobilize others, so that they have the chance to learn and grow. Acts of leadership should aim to inspire employees to build new skills and capacities, encouraging them to invest in and increase their strengths. This nurtures a learning and collaborative environment.

Mistakes happen. Encourage your employees and yourself to learn from mistakes. The environment should not be one in which mistakes are despised, but one where mistakes are considered an opportunity to learn and improve. Employees are not just numbers; they are people, and prosper only when they feel fulfilled on many levels. If they feel they are learning and growing, they will be able to share their best qualities with the organization.

»

Your best teacher is your last mistake.

– Ralph Nader

«

What Comes Next?

Once you have taken a hard look at what could stand in the way of your strategy, once you have removed both the physical and psychological barriers, and once you have acquired the tools and capacities that are necessary for success, the only thing left is to actually DO IT! Execution is the next step. Though execution may seem simple enough, most of us have learned to expect surprises just around the corner, and know that even the best plans sometimes go awry.

>>

Ideas are useless unless used. The proof of their value is in their implementation. Until then, they are in limbo.

– Theodore Levitt

<<

THE PDG MODEL

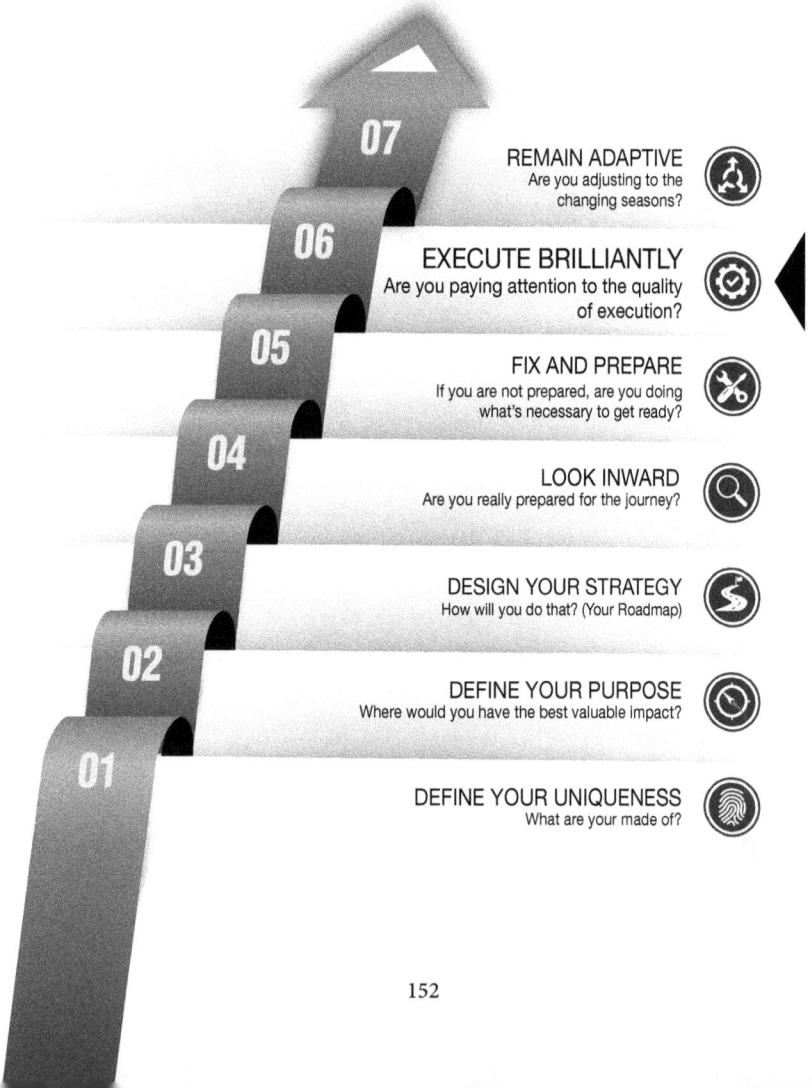

07 REMAIN ADAPTIVE
Are you adjusting to the
changing seasons?

06 EXECUTE BRILLIANTLY
Are you paying attention to the quality
of execution?

05 FIX AND PREPARE
If you are not prepared, are you doing
what's necessary to get ready?

04 LOOK INWARD
Are you really prepared for the journey?

03 DESIGN YOUR STRATEGY
How will you do that? (Your Roadmap)

02 DEFINE YOUR PURPOSE
Where would you have the best valuable impact?

01 DEFINE YOUR UNIQUENESS
What are your made of?

CHAPTER SIX

EXECUTE
BRILLIANTLY

> Strategy is a commodity, execution is an art.
>
> *– Peter Drucker*

You have identified your uniqueness, you have defined your purpose, and you have planned a strategy to move towards fulfilling that purpose. You have taken the time to discover the physical and psychological aspects that may block your organization from realizing your strategy, and fixed those that were evident at the time. You have also spent some time acquiring the necessary capacities to enable the implementation.

Execution is crucially important and should not be sidelined or disregarded just because you have an inspiring purpose or compelling strategy. Execution makes everything come together. It's sometimes a trial and error period. Your carefully laid plans need to be tried and tested, and eventually adjusted to better fit with reality. It is not a quick process. It often takes companies years to establish a stride that can lead to success.

>>

You show me a successful complex system, and I will show you a system that has evolved through trial and error.

– Tim Harford

<<

Choosing The Right People To Lead

>>

To succeed consistently, good managers need to be skilled not just in choosing, training, and motivating the right people for the right job, but in choosing, building, and preparing the right organization for the job as well.

– Clayton Christensen

<<

In one company I worked for, there was a point where shareholders decided to get consultants to draw a growth plan for one of the company's subsidiaries. They insisted that the company assign one of the managers they felt would be good for the job to oversee the execution of that strategy. Unfortunately, he was the wrong choice. He was an excellent strategist, he could see the bigger picture, and the ideas he came up with were remarkable, but when it came to the micro level, he did not have the right skills to execute the strategy.

The execution part requires follow-up and attention to detail, making sure everything is communicated well, and implemented properly. It involves leadership skills that are field-based. This manager failed to execute the most essential task – hiring the right people – and the operation failed.

To truly lead in execution, you must embody the maestro of an orchestra. Each element of the strategy must work with the other elements to produce harmony. Unfortunately, this manager would qualify more as a composer than a maestro. Therefore, the project dragged on and was met with great dissatisfaction and cost.

Here is a contrasting example. In a major cable television network company where I was the CEO, we were once faced with a crisis that entailed relocating our entire transmission infrastructure to another country in one month. This was not an easy feat. Nonetheless, the execution plan was put into place, and it entailed moving a farm of huge satellite signal receivers and transmitters.

To our delight, the individual in charge of the execution managed to make the move without any major problems. The viewers did not notice any interruptions, and he and his team completed the move before the allocated deadline. He was even able to cut costs, as he used creative and adaptive methods when problems arose. Despite the immensity of the project, it was carried out with skill and finesse.

Without the right people implementing the strategy, you will have failed before you even begin. The people who are responsible for implementation are at the core of the strategy's success, so they must be carefully chosen.

This cannot be stressed enough. The roles need to be assigned wisely and thoughtfully, playing to each individual's strengths and weaknesses. In the first example, the chosen manager was not meant to execute a strategy, but to create one. His specialty lay in viewing things from a macro level, not planning the minute details and the implementation process. In contrast, in the second example, the individual in charge knew exactly what he had to do, and he was therefore able to orchestrate the whole process without major hiccups.

Usually, implementing the strategy will require creating different roles, each with specific tasks. It is crucial that you choose the right people to play those roles. To do this, you will need to consider three aspects:

The first is the "Hand". The person you wish to assign to a specific role must have the required technical competencies to get the job done. The first manager in the examples above did not have the right skills to fulfill the duties of the role he was assigned to.

The second is the "Head". Implementing a strategy will require the implementer to think critically about the most efficient and effective ways to progress. If the implementation phase experiences hiccups and setbacks, the person tasked with a specific role needs to be able to deal with the problems that arise. They must exhibit creativity, innovation, and problem-solving abilities, among other things. Consider the second manager in the examples above. He had the right analytical mind for the job. He was creative in the implementation, finishing ahead of the deadline, and he resolved the problems he encountered without inconveniencing the customers.

Finally, the "Heart". Different roles will require different sets of values, not including the organization's core values. Some roles will require speed, others efficiency, and others precision. You need to be clear on what values are necessary for the specific job, and then examine whether the person tasked with the job has them. For instance, you need to hire someone meticulous, conscientious, and strict to oversee quality control at an aircraft manufacturing company.

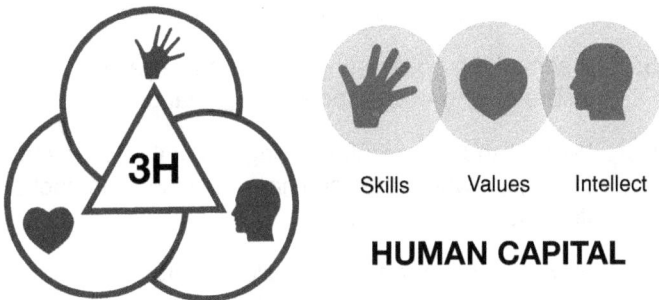

Skills   Values   Intellect

HUMAN CAPITAL

Figure 6.1:
General model of recruitment

Choosing the right people to lead a part of the execution is crucial. Before assigning them their respective roles, ensure that they fit all three aspects. Having a person with the right hand, head, and heart increases the chances of the strategy succeeding. The capabilities of the people in different roles must synchronize with their respective duties in the implementation phase.

Each role assigned to individuals should be clear and concise.

Questions:

1. What role does each person play?

2. What is being done to ensure that they aware of their responsibilities?

3. How clear are the expectations and consequences?

4. Is time being taken to identify who makes recommendations and offers input, who makes decisions, and who implements those decisions?

5. If something goes wrong, how is management made aware of who was responsible for that operation?

6. What is the organization doing to put its best people in the jobs where they can have the biggest impact on its strategic decisions?

7. How can the organization build leadership capacities among its people? How can it help them develop the appropriate skills and knowledge to implement the strategy?

Coordination

As well as ensuring the right people are put in positions of leadership, it is also important to have processes in place that help the different parts of the organization work together well – so they can coordinate.

Coordination is a key part of implementation, especially if the strategy involves a large number of departments and employees. As the number of people involved increases, the risk of something going awry in the execution phase will increase too. Without coordination, the execution of the strategy is more likely to fail.

Let us again consider the orchestra analogy. It is the maestro's responsibility to make sure that the orchestra plays in harmony. The different musicians must play their parts well, but they also need to be able to coordinate with their fellow musicians. If one player plays their piece well but at the wrong time, there will be chaos. The responsibility is on all the musicians to be mindful of the timing and harmony.

The same applies to executing a strategy. Remember that the strategy needs to be aligned with purpose and is often an organization-wide effort. There needs to be coordination between the different parts for the puzzle to be completed. Even if each individual or department carried out their role flawlessly, the strategy would not be fully implemented until the different parts came together.

Questions:

1. What coordination systems does your organization have?

2. Is coordination a key part of the organizational culture? How does your organization highlight the importance of coordination?

3. Are the people or groups responsible for the coordination efforts competent enough? What is your organization doing to ensure that those responsible have the necessary capacities?

Collaboration

Once you have considered coordination and ensured that different groups can work well together, it's time to think about collaboration. The individuals involved in the strategy must also be able to collaborate effectively.

If the people who are executing the strategy cannot work together, the execution phase will be challenging. Remember that implementing the strategy is a collective effort, so it is of paramount importance that the people responsible for executing it be able to coordinate and collaborate.

For instance, in an orchestra, different musicians

may be able to play their part in a professional and timely manner, but if they are unable to collaborate with their fellow musicians, it will negatively affect the harmony and spoil the piece of music.

Collaboration is central to problem-solving. When the organization encounters a problem, the people responsible for solving it may fail if they are unable to work harmoniously with one another. They may not see eye to eye on solutions, and might be more prone to finger-pointing and individualist mentalities than teamwork. The organization must resolve existing and potential collaborative issues before beginning the implementation phase, otherwise they risk leaving issues unsolved and possibly harming the execution of the strategy.

Creativity takes a hit when people in a work group compete instead of collaborate.

Teresa Amabile

Questions:

1. Do the different people and groups in your organization work well together when executing the strategy? If not, what can your organization do to help them harmonize?

2. Is collaboration a key part of the organizational culture? How is your organization highlighting its importance?

3. When your organization encounters problems, how do your employees work collectively to solve them?

4. What can you or your organization do to improve collaboration among different people in the organization?

5. What measures can your organization take to ensure that the execution team can and will collaborate when implementing strategies?

Communication

During the implementation phase, communication also plays a crucial role. It is a key building block of coordination and collaboration. People or departments communicate with one another to help ensure that the different parts of the system are working together harmoniously. Communication is also about ensuring the flow of data, information, knowledge, ideas, and feedback. Good communication increases the chances that the strategy will be successfully executed.

Communication is important for strategic planning to be translated into implementation. With an effective communication system in place, the people responsible for formulating the strategy can communicate its details to those tasked with implementing it. If the people in the field don't know or understand the details of the strategy, or do not completely understand their roles and responsibilities, they will be unable to successfully carry out the plan. Furthermore, the people implementing the strategy must communicate with one another as they execute the plan.

Remember, a strategic plan that is not well executed will waste valuable resources, and prevent an organization from fulfilling its purpose. There might not be enough resources available for a second implementation attempt or a new strategy.

Therefore, it is of paramount importance that open communication be given priority in the execution phase. It must become part of the organization's culture, even before the implementation phase begins. All the information that people need to successfully execute the strategy must be communicated, and at times over-communicated. It is better to repeat the plan time and time again than to risk people not understanding it fully.

The flow of information is fundamental for the organization to run as smoothly as possible. When all the information is presented properly, second-guessing and indecisiveness will be infrequent. Communication channels should be open at all times so that signals are not mixed.

Communication also helps when issues arise during the execution phase. When there is a problem in one area, it may affect another area of the strategy, which in turn may affect the strategy overall. When there are open channels of communication, people can let others know that issues have occurred in their respective parts. This will allow for collective problem-solving, ensuring that progress is not hindered.

Think about a construction site. It is important that there is an open channel of communication between different people working on the project. They must know what they are expected to do, when they are expected to work, and who to report to. They must have all the plans and blueprints at hand. If one of the subcontractors encounters a problem, they need to be able to communicate to the rest of the teams to let them know, otherwise they will delay the project, or possibly make a mistake that undoes progress.

Questions:

1. What is your organization doing to encourage and prioritize communication?

2. How can your organization build a culture that fosters open communication?

3. Is your organization effectively communicating the plan to those responsible for implementing it?

4. What channels are set up to ease communication between different people in your organization?

5. Have there been issues in the execution phase that can be attributed to a lack of proper communication? What should be done to improve communication in your organization?

6.   In what ways have open channels of communication helped your organization grow?

Attention to Detail

During strategic planning, the organization should spend time working out a detailed plan for every step of the strategy process, ironing out any creases and searching for problems before initiating anything. When it is time to put the strategy into action, it is crucial that the organization pays attention to this plan to ensure the smoothest possible execution.

Unfortunately, at times, organizations will experience certain pressures (e.g. deadlines, shortage of resources, unexpected interruptions and delays) that will affect how much detail they can apply when carrying out the strategy. They may decide to skimp on certain intricacies for the sake of cost or finishing on the agreed upon deadline, but this can have consequences. Attention to detail can be the determining factor of quality in the implementation of the strategy.

The organization needs to clearly communicate the importance of following the strategy down to the last detail. It needs to make sure that there are no compromises or shortcuts when it comes to executing the strategy.

Consider the way that pilots have a checklist to go through before, during, and after the flight. No matter how experienced a pilot is, she must still go through even the most boring and routine details to ensure that all systems and protocols are in order. This helps decrease the chance of a crash due to overlooked mistakes.

Possible reasons for organizations to forego the details are:

- **Poor planning.** It is possible that during the formulation of the strategy, the intricacies were not given as much importance as they deserved. Therefore, the blueprint from which the organization is working is not elaborate enough.

- **Lack of Monitoring Systems.** Some parts of the system may compromise on details for the sake of finishing faster, increasing quantity, or because they are facing pressure from other stakeholders. Without monitoring systems in place to check up on the different steps in the process, the details may not be given the importance they deserve, and this may negatively affect the organization in the long-run.

- **Lack of Proper Communication.** It is possible that the strategy was not communicated in its entirety to the people implementing the strategy, or they may have misunderstood it. Without a clear understanding, the implementation of the strategy may not be detailed enough to be successful.

Questions:

1. How does your organization highlight the importance of paying attention to the intricacies of a project?

2. What type of industry is your organization in? Does it rely heavily on attention to detail?

3. Has your organization experienced failures due to lack of care? What systems are in place to stop such failures from being repeated?

4. Are there systems in place to ensure attention to detail receives the focus it deserves? If not, then what can you or your organization do to create and adopt such systems?

Monitoring Capabilities

How can your organization know if the strategy is going according to plan? Part of the implementation phase requires that systems be in place to monitor the progress of the strategy. Before beginning with the execution, the organization needs to spend some time setting these up.

These systems will allow the organization to assess how different parts are handling the execution. If there is any part of the organization that is negatively affecting the progress of the strategy, the organization can pinpoint it and deal with it accordingly.

With a strong monitoring system in place, an organization can also keep an eye on the details and specifics of different stages in the strategy. People are less likely to take shortcuts or make negative compromises if they know that they are being monitored.

Monitoring systems will hold people accountable for their goals and respective responsibilities in the execution of the strategy. Whether the systems pick up on mistakes or successful progress, having such systems in place will allow the organization to reward or reprimand people.

Possible monitoring systems include: progress reports, individual and group milestones, random inspections, etc.

Questions:

1. Does your organization have effective monitoring processes in place? What are they?

2. Is the execution of plans closely monitored? How?

3. What accountability guidelines does your organization have in place? How are people held accountable for fulfilling their responsibilities and meeting expectations?

Improvisation

During the implementation phase, there is a chance that the strategy will experience some unplanned bumps; there will be situations that the strategy did not anticipate. Although these might not pose a major problem, they are still obstacles that may require a change, small or large, in the direction or strategy. The system needs to improvise and work with any new, relevant information that surfaces during the execution of the strategy.

People responsible for carrying out the plan need to be able to improvise whenever they encounter unplanned situations, otherwise the organization will end up sticking to a strategy that simply cannot be applied successfully, and this will increase the chances that the strategy will fail.

For instance, technology is currently advancing at a phenomenal rate. It is possible that while an organization is implementing a strategy, a new technology will be released on the market that would increase efficiency and accuracy, or that is more eco-friendly. The organization may need to improvise and adapt their plan to include this new technology, especially if the strategy is intended for the long-term.

Implementing the strategy is not a rigid process, but a dynamic one. The organization must be prepared to make changes and improvise when necessary.

Questions:

1. How is your organizational environment conducive to improvisation and adaptation? How much opportunity are your employees given to improvise?

2. How open are the employees in your organization to taking purposeful, calculated risks? Do they welcome improvisation?

3. What can your organization do to encourage purposeful improvisation?

Contingency Planning

During the implementation phase, some external or internal changes may call for abandoning either the whole or part of the implementation plan. In such situations, the organization may need to resort to a contingency plan – a back-up plan – to fulfill its goals.

Contingency plans come in the form of "if-then" or "what if" scenarios. During strategic planning, the organization may spend some time considering what likely scenarios might threaten the smooth implementation of the strategy, and what could be done to mitigate the risks posed by these scenarios.

If the scenario then occurs, the organization can refer to their contingency plans and adopt one that suits the situation. This way, the execution will proceed, even when the original plan is disrupted.

Even once the execution phase has begun, an organization should construct contingency plans based on new information or changes in the environment. Predicting and preempting problems that would require big changes allows an organization to ride these changes with minimal risk to progress and resources.

Questions:

1. What possible issues might arise during the implementation of your strategy? Do you have contingency plans in place to deal with these possible issues? If not, what contingency plans would address them?

2. How does your organization communicate these plans to its members?

3. What can your organization do to ensure that the execution team is capable of applying the contingency plans when necessary?

4. Is contingency thinking part of your organizational culture? How can your organization incorporate it into its culture?

Problem Solving Ability

As well as having contingency plans, your organization should be well-equipped for dealing with situation where there is no plan yet, or when the plan does not work.

If the strategy reaches a standstill, the organization must have systems in place to diagnose the problem, solve it, and refocus its efforts on implementing the strategy.

If they discover that they are dealing with a physical challenge, they must consider what resources and expertise are required to successfully resolve it. Are the wrong people leading the implementation? Do they need more resources? Do they have the right capacities?

If an organization realizes that it is dealing with a psychological challenge, it must diagnose its causes quickly. For instance, if some of the key people in the organization were originally against the strategy, they might use the implementation phase as an opportunity to sabotage the execution and the strategy overall. To solve the problem, the organization may opt to remove them from the implementation team, or deal with the core reasons of their continued resistance.

There are also legal, financial, environmental, security, and political problems, as well as others, which might arise. The organization needs to be prepared to deal with such challenges, or else they risk the success of the execution phase.

Questions:

1. How is your organization equipped to solve problems? What problem solving abilities do the employees of your organization have?

2. What systems are in place to help your organization accurately diagnose problems when they arise?

3. What does your organization do to promote individual problem solving? What about collective problem solving?

4. How can your organization help its people build the necessary capacities and develop problem solving abilities?

Practical Intelligence

A strategy can make sense on paper, but sometimes when it comes to implementation, it might prove challenging. Implementing a strategy will require practical intelligence – the ability to consider creative hands-on solutions to unexpected problems. There may be moments when the plan is simply not practical, and the person executing the strategy will need to consider how s/he can achieve its goal in a pragmatic way.

A person who has practical intelligence will inspect their environment, consider what resources they have at hand, and find the most realistic solution to the issue. Practical intelligence is beneficial because there will be moments in the implementation phase where they don't have the luxury of time, and they need to find a solution on the spot. In these cases, people draw on their practical knowledge to resolve the problem without hindering the progress of the strategy.

Questions:

1. In what instances do the employees of your organization exhibit practical intelligence?

2. How can your organization offer its employees enough practical experience to improve their practical intelligence?

Creativity

Creativity is the ability to come up with novel and original ideas, tools, practices, and solutions that increase value creation, sometimes building on and enhancing conventional ideas and practices. Creativity can be applied on two levels.

Firstly, it can be applied in the planning phase, where innovative ideas can be introduced to the plan, surpassing conventional and mainstream thinking. Secondly, creativity can be applied in the implementation phase, where unusual thinking and new approaches could be applied to the execution.

In some organizations, the people on the field are given freedom to be creative – they have authority's permission – when implementing the strategy, provided their creative solutions comply with the organization's purpose, its values, and the guidelines set forth by the strategy. They can choose to adopt standard ways to implement specific tasks, or they can choose to experiment with new ideas, depending on which benefits the execution of the strategy.

In the implementation phase, creativity can mean the difference between a successful execution and a failed one. There will be times when the tried and tested methods do not apply. This might be due to changes in the circumstances, or the fact that the people executing the plan found that the older methods were no longer as effective. For instance, technological advancements change how efficiently an organization can complete certain tasks. Introducing machines to take over manual tasks during the Industrial Revolution is one such example.

At times, proposed creative solutions may not achieve the desired results, and the workers will need to consider sticking to more conventional methods. At other times, a novel solution will prove successful, possibly helping cut costs, increase efficiency, and offer more value.

For example, during the implementation phase of a governmental preservation strategy, the people responsible for executing the plan decide to stop using expensive satellite imagery to monitor the forests. They chose to use drones instead, which offered a cheaper and more frequent way of monitoring activity.

Creativity can also be applied to problem solving. When issues arise, an organization needs to improvise, and creativity can play a defining role. People executing the strategy may choose to experiment, through trial and error, with different ways of dealing with the problem.

Questions:

1. To what extent does your organization belong to an industry that allows for creative practices and solutions?

2. How does your organization's culture support creative initiatives? How does it empower and encourage its employees to make decisions when implementing the strategy?

3. What systems are in place to allow for creative solutions and ideas to be communicated through different levels of your organization?

Resourcefulness

Resourcefulness is also a crucial part of the implementation phase. It is one thing to consider creative solutions; it is another to implement them.

Resourcefulness is about finding the most skillful way to implement the creative plan and deal with an issue or new situation. It is crucial to the implementation phase, especially when you consider that often an organization will be pressed for time and resources. With resourcefulness, the people responsible for implementing the strategy can creatively deal with problems and make the best use of the assets at their disposal.

With a resourceful mindset, the people responsible will be more willing to question what can and cannot be done, surpassing limitations, and efficiently and skillfully moving the implementation phase along. This mindset will allow the organization to take a deeper look into the available resources and see if they can be put to better use.

For instance, imagine an organization has a fixed deadline to finish coding a specific computer program, and they are understaffed. One of the people responsible for the project looks for solutions within the organization, and she finds that a couple of employees in the accounting department are skilled programmers. She decides to give them temporary access and responsibility for working alongside the IT department. This allows them to deal with the pressure and hand in the project on time.

Resourcefulness also draws on practical intelligence. The know-how and experience of dealing with problems which the people in the field often have – practical intelligence – allows them to find the most creative, efficient, and pragmatic solutions.

Questions:

1. How do your employees exhibit resourcefulness when it comes to dealing with challenges?

2. How is your organization able to make the best use of its resources? What difficulties does it face due to the constraints of limited resources?

3. What can you do to encourage a culture of resourcefulness in your organization?

Crisis Management

Another crucial part of the implementation phase is crisis management. Crises are usually sudden changes that destabilize the situation, and that need to be handled in order to restore the previous equilibrium. They are not small anomalies, but rather abnormal situations that need to be normalized. These things are likely to happen during the implementation of plans.

Crisis management is about setting up behavioral protocols and safeguards. These must be communicated in advance to individuals within the organization, so they have a guideline to follow in the event of a crisis. In some instances, an incident can be stopped from developing into a crisis if there are proper communication, coordination, and collaboration systems set up.

In addition to this, crisis management is needed when the crisis is wholly unexpected and catches the organization by surprise. In this case, there may not be clear cut ways of dealing with the aftermath. The organization will have to act fast and come up with a solution on the spot. This can be quite challenging as they will be under pressure, without clearly articulated and thought-out guidelines, and without having all the information to come up with the proper solutions. They will need to improvise and make snap judgments.

For example, imagine a museum in a city that does not usually encounter earthquakes. An earthquake occurs that cracks the walls of the museum, and the water pipes burst. Water begins to flood on the paintings and art pieces. In this unexpected situation, there are no guidelines, and the museum staff will need to think of solutions quickly, otherwise the art pieces will be at risk of being permanently lost.

Therefore, it is important that an organization take the time to set up protocols in the case of an emergency, and that if there are none, the staff are able to think of quick solutions to (sometimes temporarily) respond to the urgent situation.

Questions:

1. Does your organization have a crisis management mentality? What can your organization do to encourage such a mentality?

2. What are your organizational protocols for dealing with crises?

3. Thinking back to a crisis your organization went through. How did it handle it?

4. What lessons could be learned from past crises?

Resilience

The tensions, setbacks and crises which implementing a strategy can cause also intensify the importance of resilience. These pressures may, at times, lead the organization to question whether the strategy is worth its effort and resources. They may even be so damaging to the organization that it chooses to abandon the strategy.

There are occasions when an organization needs to completely revolutionize its strategy, but it is vital that it does not give up prematurely. Exhibiting resilience is crucial if an organization is to endure setbacks and failures when things don't go according to plan, or to push back against resistance when tensions are high. The people responsible for executing the strategy must be able to take a hit, and in some cases stumble, but get back up and move forward.

A resilient execution team needs to consider how to make the best out of a bad situation. They must reflect on setbacks or resistance, learn, and find ways to turn negatives into positives which will enhance the strategy and its implementation.

For example, SpaceX experienced many setbacks before one of its rockets succeeded in reaching the earth's orbit. It also took until 2015 for a rocket to land back on the ground intact. SpaceX's willingness to get back up, learn from their mistakes, and try again is the embodiment of a resilient organization, especially as they experienced many costly setbacks and disappointments.

Resilience is a key strength that an organization must cultivate to increase the chances of a successful implementation.

Questions:

1. How resilient is your organization? How can you give resilience greater importance?

2. What can your organization do to encourage a resilient culture?

3. When your organization dealt with setbacks or tension in the past, how did it react? Did it give up or push back?

Values Guidelines

During the look inward step, the organization spent time identifying its core and aspired values. At this point, it should be clear what values the organization wishes to uphold and incorporate into its culture. These values will fall in line with the organization's purpose.

Purpose and values set the parameters of what is acceptable and what is not, what is important and what is not. The strategy is planned around these parameters.

In the implementation phase, an organization must ensure that executing the strategy is in accordance with these values.

Different organizations can have different priorities and values. For example, in one of the organizations that I led throughout my career, the prime value was "quality comes first". In another, "safety comes first", and in another, "speed comes first".

As we have seen, during the execution process, an organization may face a reality that it did not expect, which can put pressures on the organization. These pressures could come from deadlines, shareholders, unexpected crises, failed plans, etc. When the implementation process is stressed, it may pressure the organization to compromise on their values, or bend these values to suit the sudden new reality.

Core values are crucial, and they form part of the organization's identity. In the execution phase, these values need to strictly be adhered to, especially when the organization is under pressure. There can be no shortcuts, otherwise the identity, brand, reputation and even the integrity of an organization's purpose might be tarnished. In this case, leadership and authority play a role in ensuring that the core values that define the organization are adhered to in every situation.

»

The lesson I learned from this is that it's easier to hold to your principles %100 of the time than it is to hold to them %98 of the time.

– Clayton Christensen

«

Questions:

1. What values does your organization hold?

2. How does your organization enforce its distinct value guidelines?

3. How clearly does it communicate these values to those responsible for executing the strategy?

4. How strict is your organization about adhering to these value guidelines?

Quality Controls

To ensure that the organization maintains the level of quality it wants to associate its product and services with, it needs to implement systems that specifically monitor quality. It also needs to make quality a core value in the organizational culture. Remember that the brand of an organization is associated with the perception of the value it offers its customers. To build up the brand, the organization needs to be consistent in the product/service it is offering, and a part of the product/ services includes its quality.

For instance, in October 2018, flight 610 of the Indonesian airline Lion Air crashed in the Java sea due to a technical malfunction. Investigations found that this issue had been noticed on several earlier flights, and yet the plane was cleared for take-off. Had there been stricter quality protocols in place, this issue would have been identified and addressed before the plane was cleared for flight. In such situations, loosening up quality controls can have dire consequences – the lives of 189 people were claimed in the crash.

Implementing the strategy is no excuse to forego quality. The organization needs to factor regular quality checks into every step of the execution, otherwise they risk the success of the strategy.

Questions:

1. What are the quality control mechanisms in the organization? How strictly are they enforced?

2. How important is quality to your organization's culture?

3. How can your organization improve the execution of its strategy?

The Road To Maintain

>>

Having a strategy in the first place is hard. Maintaining a strategy is even harder.

– Michael Porter

<<

Even once you have brilliantly implemented your strategy and the organizational objectives have been achieved, the challenges of survival and growth are endless. You, your people, your organization, and the surrounding environment are constantly changing. What has worked so far might not be relevant if the reality changes. As the saying goes, "what got you here might not get you there." That is why adaptation is so vital to survival and growth.

You need to always return to the drawing board. The PDG Model is a continuous process. You need to constantly ask:

1. Does your uniqueness still stand?

2. Is the purpose still meaningful?

3. Are the choices you made when designing your strategies still valid?

4.   What do your organization's key performance
     indicators say about its well-being?

5.   What physical or psychological fixes need to be
     introduced to deal with the new realities?

6.   How can you ensure a good execution of your
     adapted plans?

THE PDG MODEL

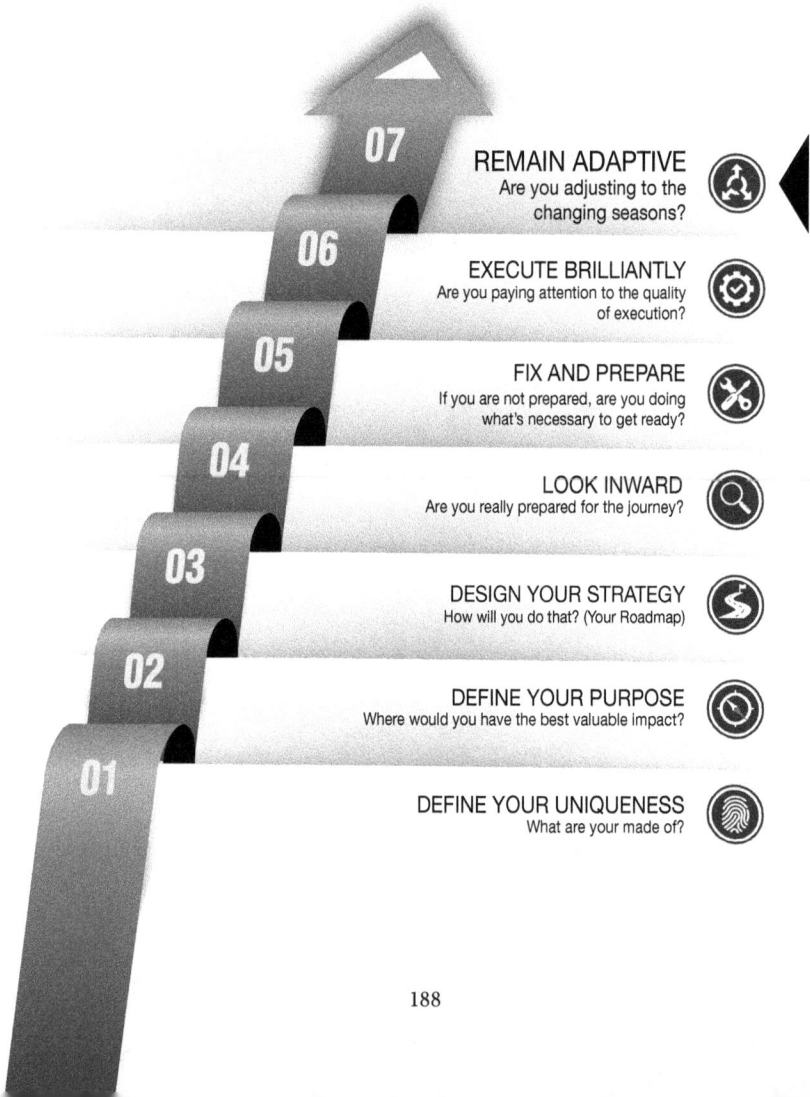

07 REMAIN ADAPTIVE
Are you adjusting to the changing seasons?

06 EXECUTE BRILLIANTLY
Are you paying attention to the quality of execution?

05 FIX AND PREPARE
If you are not prepared, are you doing what's necessary to get ready?

04 LOOK INWARD
Are you really prepared for the journey?

03 DESIGN YOUR STRATEGY
How will you do that? (Your Roadmap)

02 DEFINE YOUR PURPOSE
Where would you have the best valuable impact?

01 DEFINE YOUR UNIQUENESS
What are your made of?

CHAPTER SEVEN

REMAIN ADAPTIVE

Intelligence is the ability to adapt to change.

– Stephen Hawking

Are you adjusting to the changing seasons?

Remaining adaptive is about enjoying the success of your organization while preparing for change. When those in charge get too comfortable, when success seems to them to be a given, their organization is in danger. The future is rarely predictable, especially in this new technological age. One day people will love a product; the next day the product is old news and people have moved on to the next thing.

Companies can get too caught up in the false sense of security offered by success. As people engage in their daily work, they rarely expect a tornado (literal or figurative) to hit, but these things do happen. We have a natural tendency to assume that bad things will happen to others, but not to us. Your culture, your employees, and your management systems must be strong enough to recalibrate and deal with whatever comes.

> If you defer investing your time and energy until you see that you need to, chances are it will already be too late.
>
> *– Clayton Christensen*

This step is the final one because it mostly involves maintaining what you have already worked so hard to achieve. If you have arrived at this stage, pat yourself on the back, and then look at what you can do to ensure your hard work thus far does not go to waste.

The PDG Model Is Continuous

The environment is not static. You must see the PDG Model as a process that repeats itself as the times change. You need to continuously examine the environment, and with every change, you need to revisit the different steps of the process. Sanity checks are part of the journey of survival and growth, and by extension the PDG Model. To remain adaptive, you should constantly return to the model.

Does your uniqueness still stand?

You must again examine your uniqueness. Does it still hold in the changed reality? Does it still give your organization a competitive advantage? If not, you will need to reconsider it. It needs to adapt to ensure your continued survival and growth. You must reexamine your organization and understand how you can update your organization's uniqueness to continue creating and adding remarkable value. That is why successful organizations have a pipeline of ideas that will ensure they have a continuous competitive advantage.

What is unique today will become tomorrow's standards

There is then a third question that you need to consider: have other organizations begun to follow in your footsteps? It might be the case that other organizations, especially your competitors, have seen the competitive value of your organization's uniqueness and have decided to imitate you. If you find yourself in this situation, you will need to consider how to reinforce your uniqueness so that it can evolve and maintain your organization's competitive advantage.

Intellectual property has the shelf life of a banana.

– Bill Gates

Is the purpose still meaningful?

Next, you must reconsider your purpose. Does it still offer meaning? Does it still echo your organization's uniqueness? Again, if you answer "yes", then little change may be needed.

If the answer to the first question is "no", if you find that your purpose no longer provides meaning, then it must adapt.

In the event that your uniqueness has changed, your purpose will need to change too. It must mirror your uniqueness so that it can differentiate the value you offer from that of other organizations. If it does not echo your organization's uniqueness, it will not offer the exceptional value that gives you a competitive advantage. As such it will also fail to offer meaning to the activities of your stakeholders, and this will negatively affect your organization's survival and growth.

Remember that your uniqueness need not always be clear before you define your organization's purpose. There are times purpose defines what an organization's uniqueness will be. As your purpose adapts, you may need to figure out how your organization can redefine its uniqueness to help fulfill your adapted purpose.

Are the choices you made when designing your strategies still valid?

Purpose guides strategy. If your organization's purpose changes, so do your organization's options, and the choices your organization must make. Furthermore, strategy formulation is based on the environment. The dynamic nature of the environment will call for changes and, at times, these changes can be disruptive. The different kinds of disruptions include: technological, political, legal, financial, environmental, among others.

Based on the changes in the environment and the new reality, ask yourself these questions:

1. What new options are open to my organization?

2. Are my major choices (i.e. strategies) still my best "best guess"?

3. Based on the new data, what different set of options do I need to consider? What are the different choices that I may need to make?

When you reexamine the changing environment, try to gather as much data as you can. If you don't understand the changes and interpret the reality correctly, your organization cannot adapt.

Let us take this a step further. Explore what opportunities and threats your strategy is currently designed to address. What current and expected opportunities and threats will you have to deal with in the new reality? Are they the same? If the threats and opportunities are changing, how can you adapt your strategy accordingly? The more accurate your reading of reality is, the clearer your options and the better your choices may be.

What do your organization's key performance indicators say about its well-being?

Your organization is a living, breathing entity and, just like you, it is always changing. Part of being adaptive involves keeping an eye on the external environment, but another part involves keeping an eye on the internal environment – your organization. You need to look into your organization, and diagnose how it has evolved with the new reality. Study its vital signs, examine how it is doing. When you look inward, you need to consider if you are still the same.

1. Are your strengths the same? Are they still strengths?

2. Are your weaknesses still weaknesses? Have they changed? Has your organization been able to leverage them and benefit from them? Can it continue to do so?

It is also possible that somewhere along the way your organization lost some of its strengths or developed new ones. An old weakness may have been overcome, or even turned into a strength that can contribute to your competitive advantage.

Remain aware of your organization. Check its vital signs. Is the heart still beating strongly? Do you have enough muscles? Have you accumulated too much fat? Are you still flexible? Are you fit for sprints or marathons?

What physical and psychological fixes need to be introduced to deal with the new realities?

Once you have diagnosed a new reality, it is time to act on this diagnosis. If your diagnosis shows that your organization has a new weakness, you will have to take measures to address it. On the other hand, if the diagnosis shows that you have acquired new strengths, you will need to consider how you can build and capitalize on them.

This step is about turning the diagnosis of the previous step into a set of action points, to ensure that you act according to the best interests of your survival and growth. You will need to exercise leadership to help your organization navigate the new reality.

Consider this as an example of problems which might arise from a new reality: your organization has grown and expanded geographically, but you are starting to experience communication issues. By analyzing the new reality, you will be able to see how the expansion has brought about a need for better communication systems. This issue was non-existent when your organization was still located in one area and everyone could speak directly to each other. You will need to adapt and take measures to fix this issue so that your organization can continue to function effectively and ensure its continued survival and growth.

On the other hand, it is possible that after your diagnosis you might realize that your expansion allows you the capacity to deliver a wider range of products and services to a wider market (where you have presence on a larger scale). This reality did not exist earlier, and you will need to take measures to capitalize on this new strength.

In times of change ask:

1. How should we overcome our weaknesses? Can we leverage them in our favor?

2. How can we build and capitalize on our strengths?

3. How can we acquire the relevant capacities to handle our new reality?

How can you ensure a good execution of your adapted plans?

As you adapt to the new reality, the steps of the PDG Model prior to execution may change. Subsequently, the strategy that you will need to implement may also change. In this case, the execution will need to adapt to suit this updated strategy.

However, the guidelines of proper execution (e.g. communication, attention to detail, etc.) remain the same. Your organization must still maintain the same principles and standards of excellence when implementing the newly adapted strategy – the one based on the new reality.

The main thing that changes in this step is that the execution needs to adapt to the changes that the new reality brings to the strategy, the organization, and the surrounding environment.

The bottom line is that remaining adaptive requires continuous learning: it does not end. The dynamic nature of the environment must be echoed by your organization's adaptive and learning culture. With the change there are often opportunities for your organization to grow. This all involves experimentation, trial and error, new ways of thinking, and possibly new interpretations and mindsets. You may need to rearrange your values, and maybe even follow new sets of behaviors.

Stay Humble

Keep learning; don't be arrogant by assuming that you know it all, that you have a monopoly on the truth; always assume that you can learn something from someone else.

– Jack Welch

Arrogance can be the Achilles' heel of an organization.

Some successful companies think success will last indefinitely. When such arrogance sets in, they start to believe they will always thrive. Rather than adapting as circumstances change, they conclude that it is others who must follow their example. This type of company remains fixed in its ways, refusing to change. A company that does not adapt will fail.

For example, in the 1990s, the company Nokia was booming. However, its success and reliance on the strength of its brand caused Nokia to stumble. Instead of keeping up with the times, they fell short and were crushed by Apple and Android, forcing them to sell their business.

Great leaders are humble. They know they are still learning, even once they have experienced success. They push for continuous improvement. You also must realize that, although **success mostly results from hard work, a lot of it is also down to chance and luck, which are notoriously variable.** Sooner or later, luck may abandon you, so ensure that the part of success you do have complete control over remains locked, loaded, and ready to handle any situation.

Reminding yourself how much of success comes from luck also helps to keep you humble and inclined to work hard. If arrogance starts to seep into your attitude, and if you start believing all your success stems from your own talents, you may start overreaching and forget the value of introspection.

In extreme cases, your success could have been the result of luck overcoming a flawed strategy or poor execution. If you don't value humility and you are unwilling to learn, you may be in for some nasty surprises. You might take on more projects than you can handle, and you could lose sight of your purpose.

> I predict one day that Amazon will fail. Amazon will go bankrupt.
>
> *– Jeff Bezos*

Continuity Versus Change

> The ability to change constantly and effectively is made easier by high-level continuity.
>
> *– Michael Porter*

Continuity is one of the most important things for a company to establish. It allows customers, suppliers, and other stakeholders to relate to the name and brand of the organization, building trust. With continuity comes an established form of reliability. For example, once you have a long-term relationship with suppliers, they can predict your needs ahead of time. This type of relationship takes years to form.

The longer you work on something, the more space you have to excel at it. It is only natural that, with years of trial and error under your belt, your company's efficiency will greatly increase. Continuity also lets your staff get to know, in-depth, the purpose and strategy of the company. Customers will come to trust the products or services they receive.

On the other hand, if the company constantly changes, the stakeholders will not take the company seriously. Change is not bad, but should only happen in line with the purpose, and only when required to adapt and evolve. Change for the sake of change should not be encouraged; it will just keep an organization jumping from one extreme to another.

If Apple were to bring out the same type of phone each year, their customers would have nothing to look forward to, and eventually, while the rest of the world moved forward with technology, the mobile phone that refused to change would become a forgotten fossil. However, it's equally true that Apple could not keep introducing new mobile phones every month or so, or their customers would be swamped, frustrated, and probably choose other brands.

You want to establish a consistent brand, but you must be prepared to make changes and innovate. The trick is to fine-tune your strategy to allow just the right amount of change. **A company should change enough to remain adaptive and innovative, but not so much as to lose sight of its original identity.**

Management Systems

The management systems that you set up during the initial cycle of the PDG Model should not be abandoned or neglected once your strategy has been successfully implemented.

Having management systems in place allows you to monitor your organization and the surrounding environment. This means you will be able to spot areas where you may need to make an intervention and adapt (internally or externally), so that you maintain the quality of your survival and capture opportunities for growth.

Make sure your organization is always mindful, conscious, and reflective

The Conclusion

Finally, we have made it to the conclusion of this model: redefining success. This does not mean that success will always be guaranteed. You will need to remain adaptive, coming up with different strategies depending on your predictions and the changes in your environment.

Problems will arise, but at least if you keep your mind on your purpose, producing strategies that align with it, and remain adaptive, you will be better equipped for dealing with the problems. You will also maintain a consistent level of success and growth. This form of success can only occur once all the above steps of the model are accomplished.

CHAPTER EIGHT

REDEFINING SUCCESS

You will fall. You will struggle. Getting up again makes all the difference

Those who can get up no matter how many times they fall, no matter how many times it seems there is no hope, are those who truly succeed. This concept is vital when it comes to persevering and reaching the true potential, either of an individual or of an organization. Too big a cliché? Well, it's a cliché for a reason – because it is true.

I am not saying that if you follow the PDG Model, it will all be smooth sailing. I am saying this model can be a good guide to running your business or organization, and can give you clarity and a sense of direction.

A brilliant way to adapt to a situation is knowing who you are and what your priorities are. From there, you can make sound decisions, and you will have the patience to be steadfast in pursuing and achieving your goals.

The telltale sign of a successful, happy, and growing organization is not just profit, but that the organization positively affects its stakeholders. In business, as in life, most things have a balance, so the more effort and time you put into something, the more rewards naturally result from it. The more contribution and fulfillment your organization brings to others, the more it will receive. This concept manifests time and time again, in the organizations that are considered top companies in the world.

One of the biggest obstacles to fulfillment or happiness is confusion – not knowing exactly what you want. Once your purpose is clear and you are working toward it, nothing can stand in your way.

I call this section redefining success because it is not about success in the typical sense of more money, or a bigger company. Instead, it relates success to a lasting form of success, fulfillment and growth.

The Road To Fulfillment

In order to really find happiness, you need to continue looking for opportunities that you believe are meaningful.

– Clayton Christensen

People are at the heart of any organization – employees, customers, suppliers, shareholders or investors, and the community in general. The only way an organization can truly succeed and be "happy" is to satisfy the parties involved, and convince them of the meaning and contribution the business or organization creates.

On a personal level, happiness is defined in so many different ways. Everyone wants to be happy, but few people seem to know what happiness involves. Many people mistake temporary excitement and brief moments of satisfaction for happiness.

On an organizational level, this false happiness is pursued by companies wanting fast results and focusing solely on profits. Such companies consider themselves happy when targets are achieved, but when targets are not achieved, they start to come undone. They may compromise on important values and quality for financial gains, and in the long run, not only the customers but also the other stakeholders will feel it.

People sense the difference between someone genuinely trying to help them and someone just trying to get something from them. When organizations truly project meaning and purpose and follow through with these principles at every level, their effort will inspire customer loyalty.

Organizations such as Whole Foods Market pay attention to every single detail in maintaining quality. Their customers trust the standards the company upholds, their humane way of dealing with animals, and the general respect that goes along with every interaction. All these factors contribute to their sustainability.

According to the psychologist Martin Seligman, the longest-lasting form of happiness stems from having a meaning in life. This type of happiness consists of knowing your purpose and using it to benefit something larger than yourself. In this way, you find meaning, and it can be your path to true happiness – fulfillment.

Fulfillment can occur on both the personal and organizational level.

Organizational Success And Meaning

An organization that is happy, or fulfilled, has created a dynamic and loyal relationship with every stakeholder. The organization has brought value and meaning to each of their lives.

Customers (those the organization aims to serve): Out of all the stakeholders, the **customers should be the heart of the organization.** The reason for existence of an organization is to add value to the lives of customers. If the customers have no use for you, then why are you there in the first place? A happy organization possesses a strong and loyal customer base as a result of fulfilling a need, solving a problem, or simply adding beauty to the lives of its consumers. Through innovation and creativity, the organization constantly adapts and finds ways to better serve the customers. In the end, when a customer is cared for and feels the organization provides them with meaning, they will return.

> It is a company's customers who effectively control what it can and cannot do.
>
> – *Clayton Christensen*

Employees: When employees work for an organization they feel truly cares about them, it manifests in their work. If employees are made to feel special and rewarded for their efforts, their ambition will be unlimited. If employees feel that they are making a difference with their work, bringing meaning to the lives of others, they will gain a sense of pride. If the work environment is one of **collaboration and teamwork**, they will feel that they are part of a family.

A cohesive group is one of the strongest tools for retaining employees and earning loyalty. When employees feel their decisions matter and that they can contribute and grow alongside the organization, they will put in more effort. When they enjoy what they do and are highly motivated, people around them will be affected. Customers in particular will recognize the passion and appreciate the dedication with which they perform their job.

> Employees who believe that management is concerned about them as a whole person – not just an employee – are more productive, more satisfied, more fulfilled. Satisfied employees mean satisfied customers, which leads to profitability.
>
> *– Anne M. Mulcahy*

Shareholders/Investors: If shareholders see that the customers are happy and loyal and the employees are working and pushing the limits for the prosperity of the organization, they will be happy. In general, shareholders want to make sure they are investing in something that will yield them the highest return on their investments, so when they see the organization helping others and making customers happy, they will understand that these attitudes translate to more shareholder profits. As long as shareholders feel the system works and they are receiving a good return on their investment, they will be happy.

> There are only three measurements that tell you nearly everything you need to know about your organization's overall performance: employee engagement, customer satisfaction, and cash flow.
>
> *– Jack Welch*

Suppliers: Suppliers need one thing from their clients: consistency. When organizations follow a purpose and are dependable overall, consistency will not be a problem. Suppliers benefit from a consistent relationship; they dread risky relationships that change constantly. They also benefit from knowing they are part of a chain contributing and adding value for people. The connection with a truly successful company can give suppliers a sense of meaning and pride in their work.

The Community: When an organization decides to open in a community, it must not only follow the rules and regulations of that community, but also give back in some way or another.

When all these different parts work together and align, success is inevitable. When an organization cares about the well-being of the people affected by its presence, it will do whatever it can to make these individuals happy. This concept is quite simple, but it is astonishing how many organizations fail to see it.

Care And Purpose: The Building Blocks Of Success

Replace your pursuit of success with the pursuit of contribution.

– Peter Drucker

An organization should be viewed as layers of people. For far too long, the business world has seen an organization merely as numbers, profits, and shares. This perception has slowly eroded the reputations of businesses and, ironically enough, their profits. The organizations that are stepping away from this narrow-minded thinking are finding their success to be both financial and beyond financial. When you see an organization as people and you care for their well-being, they will in turn care for the well-being of the organization. Purpose gives each stakeholder a clear direction for the organization, differentiating it from others and creating meaning. **When the stakeholders are aligned toward one purpose, the result is harmony and growth.**

»

The least of things with a meaning is worth more in life than the greatest of things without it.

– Carl Jung

«

Surviving is not easy, and thriving is even harder, but both are possible and definitely worth the effort, especially as they lead to the ultimate goal: fulfillment.

Beyond Strategy

NOTES

"About." *Google*, www.google.com/about/.

"About Harley-Davidson | Harley-Davidson UK." *Harley-Davidson USA*, www.harley-davidson.com/gb/en/about-us/company.html.

"About - Microsoft." *Microsoft*, www.microsoft.com/en-us/about.

"About Tesla | Tesla." *Tesla, Inc*, www.tesla.com/about.

Aurik, Johan C., et al. *"The State of Strategy Today."* A.T. Kearney, www.atkearney.com/strategy-and-top-line-transformation/article?/a/the-state-of-strategy-today.

Baldoni, John. "The Importance of Resourcefulness." *Harvard Business Review*, 13 Jan. 2010, hbr.org/2010/01/leaders-can-learn-to-make-do-a.

Boutelle, Clif. "Practical Intelligence Can Mean The Difference." *Society for Industrial and Organizational Psychology, Inc.*, www.siop.org/Media/News/practical.aspx.

Britton, Vicky. "5 Disney Success Tips for Start-Ups – Disney and DreamWorks – Medium." *Medium.com,* Medium, 19 May 2015, medium.com/disney-and-animation/5-disney-success-tips-for-start-ups-19aeb4ba1b67.

Burkitt, Laurie. "Home Depot Learns Chinese Prefer 'Do-It-for-Me'." *The Wall Street Journal,* Dow Jones & Company, 14 Sept. 2012, www.wsj.com/articles/SB10000872396390444433504577651072911154602.

Christensen, Clayton M., et al. "Know Your Customers' 'Jobs to Be Done.'" *Harvard Business Review,* 24 Aug. 2016, hbr.org/2016/09/know-your-customers-jobs-to-be-done.

Collins, James Charles. *How the Mighty Fall: and Why Some Companies Never Give In.* Jim Collins, 2009.

Everly, George S. "Building a Resilient Organizational Culture." *Harvard Business Review,* 23 July 2014, hbr.org/2011/06/building-a-resilient-organizat.

Fell, Jason. "How Steve Jobs Saved Apple." *Entrepreneur,* Entrepreneur, 27 Oct. 2011, www.entrepreneur.com/article/220604.

Goldfarb, Norman M. "When Patents Became Interesting in Clinical Research." *Journal of Clinical Research Best Practices,* vol. 2, no. 3, Mar. 2006.

Heifetz, Ronald A., and Martin Linsky. *Leadership on the Line: Staying Alive through the Dangers of Leading.* Harvard Business School Press, 2008.

Heifetz, Ronald, et al. *The Practice of Adaptive Leadership Tools and Tactics for Changing Your Organization and the World.* Harvard Business Press, 2009.

Jeanty, Jacquelyn. "What Is Strategic Contingency Planning?" *Small Business - Chron.com,* Chron.com, 21 Nov. 2017, smallbusiness.chron.com/strategic-contingency-planning-25052.html.

JayMJ23. "Michael Jordan "Become Legendary #4" Nike Commercial." *YouTube,* 21 Apr. 2008, www.youtube.com/watch?v=7NsCLrcPl88.

Karmini, Niniek, and David Koenig. "Report Faults Safety Failures, Defects in Lion Air Crash."*AP News,* The Associated Press, 29 Nov. 2018, www.apnews.com/4cf97e9b0a004cf5a0db401bb1d222e1.

Keller, Valerie. "The Business Case For Purpose." *Harvard Business Review.* Boston, Mass.: Harvard Business School Publishing, 2015.

Lafley, Alan G., and Roger L. Martin. *Playing to Win: How Strategy Really Works.* Harvard Business Review Press, 2013.

Lencioni, Patrick. *The Advantage: Why Organizational Health Trumps Everything Else in Business.* Jossey-Bass, 2012.

Mackey, John, and Rajendra Sisodia. *Conscious Capitalism: Liberating the Heroic Spirit of Business.* Harvard Business Review Press, 2014

Magretta, Joan. *Understanding Michael Porter: The Essential Guide to Competition and Strategy.* Harvard Business Review Press, 2012.

Martinuzzi, Bruna. "9 Ways To Improve Your Attention To Detail." *OPEN Forum,* American Express Foreign Exchange Services, 14 Jan. 2014, www.americanexpress.com/en-us/business/trends-and-insights/articles/9-ways-to-improve-your-attention-to-detail/.

"Mission Statement." *The Economist*, The Economist Newspaper, 2 June 2009, www.economist.com/news/2009/06/02/mission-statement.

"Mission, Vision & Values." *The Coca-Cola Company*, www.coca-colacompany.com/our-company/mission-vision-values.

Mourkogiannis, Nikos. *Purpose: The Starting Point of Great Companies.* Palgrave, 2006

Nicol, Will. "The Biggest Milestones in SpaceX's History." *Digital Trends,* Digital Trends, 30 Jan. 2018, www.digitaltrends.com/cool-tech/spacex-biggest-milestones/.

"Our History." *BlinkNow,* Blink Now Foundation, blinknow.org/pages/our-history.

Peterson, Andrea. "Samsung Recalls Galaxy Note 7 after Battery Explosions and Fires." *The Washington Post,* WP Company, 2 Sept. 2016, www.washingtonpost.com/news/the-switch/wp/2016/09/02/samsung-recalls-galaxy-note-7s-after-battery-explosions-and-fires/?noredirect=on&utm_term=.41ae8aac17f0.

Pink, Daniel H. *Drive*. Riverhead Books, 2009.

"Read Nike's Mission Statement and Find Information about NIKE, Inc. Innovation, Sustainability, Community Impact and More." *Nike News*, about.nike.com/.

Reiman, Joey. *The Story of Purpose: the Path to Creating a Brighter Brand, a Greater Company, and a Lasting Legacy.* Wiley, 2013.

Sinek, Simon. *Start with Why: How Great Leaders Inspire Everyone to Take Action.* Portfolio/Penguin, 2011.

"Strategy" in Welch, Jack, and Welch, Suzy. *Winning.* Harper, 2007. Some of the questions in the third chapter of this book, "Design your Strategy", have been adapted from the five slides in chapter 9 *(strategy)* of Jack And Suzy Welch's book *Winning.*

"This Is IKEA." *IKEA*, www.ikea.com/ms/en_SG/about_ikea/our_business_idea/index.html.

Welch, Jack, and Welch, Suzy. *Winning.* Harper, 2007.

Wiersma, Bill. *The Power of Professionalism.* Ravel Media, 2011.

ABOUT THE AUTHOR

Michael Kouly began his career as a Reuters war journalist. He covered armed conflicts that involved, Israel, Lebanon, Syria, Iran, Hezbullah, Islamic extremists, terrorism, the United States, Kuwait, Iraq and others... He also covered musical concerts, fashion shows and car racing.

Writing about wars, geopolitics, international diplomacy, and global events offered Michael unique opportunities to witness, analyze and write about leadership at the highest levels: where bad leadership meant the loss of thousands of lives and good leadership led to avoiding wars, saving lives and rebuilding shattered countries.

Michael also exercised corporate leadership over a period of 30 years as he led the growth of regional and international businesses. He is a three-time CEO and president at organizations like Reuters, Orbit and Cambridge Institute for Global Leadership, managing people in more than 20 countries.

Over the span of his career, Michael made some good decisions that generated remarkable success and also some not so good decisions that offered valuable lessons on what works and what doesn't when exercising leadership - emphasizing the mindset of "you either win or learn".

From as far back as he can remember, Michael has been fascinated by leadership. He has spent his life learning about leadership, purpose and strategy by practicing them, watching others lead and by conducting extensive research on the art and science of mobilizing people and organizations towards growth and noble purposes.

Michael is a World Bank Fellow, author and keynote speaker about leadership, strategy, purpose and international politics. He is the founder of the Kouly Institute and the creator of unique Executive Leadership Programs, that have been delivered to thousands of top business executives, NGO's and government leaders worldwide.

He also dedicates time to various non-profit organizations such as the Middle East Leadership Academy (MELA), Central Eurasia Leadership Academy (CELA), South East Asia Leadership Academy (SEALA) and Leaders Across Boarders (LAB).

His calling is to help people, organizations and countries lead purpose-driven lives.

Michael studied at Harvard and Princeton Universities, and is an advisor to state leaders.

OTHER BOOKS
BY THE AUTHOR

WIDE OPEN

Leadership is a dangerous enterprise, but the rewards are valuable. This book is designed to be your companion in your thrilling journey of remarkable survival and outstanding growth.

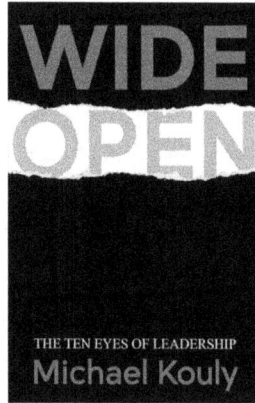

WIDE

OPEN

THE TEN EYES OF LEADERSHIP
Michael Kouly

THIS UNIQUE AND ILLUMINATING BOOK WILL OPEN YOUR EYES WIDE, SO YOU LEARN MORE ABOUT:

- **Authority:** You are surrounded by authority figures such as parents, bosses, CEOs, presidents, or governments. As you already know, not understanding how to deal with authority is risky.

- **Enemies:** Enemies are a fact of life. They could be passive or aggressive. Enemies want to undermine you and your acts of leadership. Not understanding how to deal with enemies is dangerous.

- **Understanding Yourself and Others:** It is hard to survive and grow and to lead yourself without understanding what drives your thoughts, feelings, words, actions, behaviors, dreams, and ambitions. It is impossible to lead others without understanding them first.

- **Understanding Systems:** We live and work in systems. A system can be a family, team, company, community, city, country or the world. Systems have their unique psychology and rules. Not understanding systems will put your existence and progress at risk, as you may be excluded or isolated from the group that you belong to.

HOW TO
TRUMP THE ENEMY

Some people love you and some don't. When you exercise leadership, some will support you and others will resist, oppose, obstruct, sabotage, or obsessively fight you until you lose.

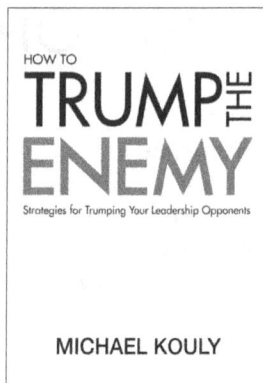

HOW TO

TRUMP THE ENEMY

Strategies for Trumping Your Leadership Opponents

MICHAEL KOULY

Most attempts at leadership fail not because of how allies are utilized, but because many leaders lack the vital skills necessary for dealing with adversaries.

What will determine your leadership success is mainly your ability to handle those who stand against you.

THIS BOOK IS A UNIQUE AND COMPREHENSIVE REFERENCE THAT YOU CAN CONSULT EVERY TIME YOU DEAL WITH RESISTERS, OPPONENTS, OR ENEMIES.

YOU WILL LEARN MORE ABOUT:

- **Strategies:** There are 104 strategies that you can use separately or in combinations as per the specific nature of the resistance that you are facing.

- **Scenarios:** There are 36 separate scenarios covering seven types of personal, social, organizational, business, and political opponents.

- **Intensities:** There are six intensities of opposition that start from passive and escalate to passive-aggressive, active, active-aggressive, malevolent, and finally archenemy.

- **You:** There is a chapter on YOU acting as your own enemy by allowing your dysfunctional mindsets, beliefs, and habits to sabotage your growth and prevent you from being all that you can be.

BOOK 1 OF THE
SELF-LEADERSHIP BOOK SERIES

FINDING YOUR HUMMUS

This book will provide you, your colleagues, family and friends with insights about life and business to unleash your personal and organizational power.

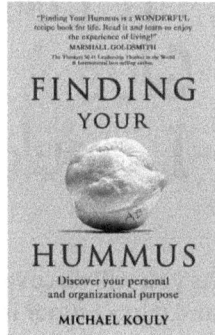

"Finding Your Hummus is a WONDERFUL recipe book for life. Read it and learn to enjoy the experience of living!"
MARSHALL GOLDSMITH
The Thinkers 50 #1 Leadership Thinker in the World & bestselling author

FINDING
YOUR
HUMMUS
Discover your personal
and organizational purpose
MICHAEL KOULY

- Shift happens in life and business, are you ready?

- What is the prime philosophy behind starting a business of growth and sustainable success?

- Do you, your people and business have a guiding purpose? This book is about finding your calling.

- Do you have a personal and organizational strategy to fulfill your purpose? This book is about self awareness, self motivation and self leadership that together can achieve self fulfillment.

- How do you deal with competition, conflict and confusion? This book is rich with empowering inspirational quotes that generate strength and lead to self actualization.

- What is the mindset to lead a life of resilience, abundance and significance? This book is about finding your passion and discovering your way of living a purpose driven life.

BOOK 2 OF THE SELF-LEADERSHIP BOOK SERIES

If I didn't
Give A ....
I would...

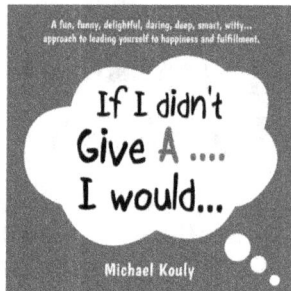

A fun, funny, delightful, daring, deep, smart, witty...
approach to leading yourself to happiness and fulfilment.

**If I didn't
Give A ....
I would...**

Michael Kouly

As you will discover, this entertaining book of insightful and witty humor is not like other self leadership books.

WHILE ENJOYING THE EXPERIENCE OF THIS BOOK, YOU'LL ALSO:

- **Blow off steam:** We all have personal issues, challenges, and obstacles that accumulate stress that must be released to keep us in a state of peak motivation.

- **Know yourself:** Sometimes an entire life is spent being stuck at the expense of personal, business, social and relational opportunities for success. Self-discovery is the first step to the healing, actualization, and optimization of your life.

- **Reflect:** Recognizing your priorities, what you really want and what matters most to you is the key to your growth in all aspects of your life.

- **Decide:** To solve problems and catch opportunities, decisions are needed. This book will help you decide and act to expand your potential in a fun, playful, smart and effective way.

- **Lead:** True leadership starts with the self where smart and effective strategy, action and execution are the keys to the growth of our capacity.

BOOK 3 OF THE
SELF-LEADERSHIP BOOK SERIES

MUTE

MICHAEL KOULY

MUTE

The voices that won't SHUT UP... and you may not know are there

It doesn't matter who you are or what you do. You carry voices in your head, voices that are always talking to you. Some of the voices whisper, others shout. Some make logical arguments, others create dramas.

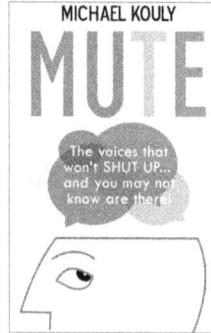

Do you know the voices in your head? Do you know where they've come from and how they are controlling you?

As soon as you meet a person, you begin to carry their voice with you. This starts with your parents, loved ones, hated ones, bosses, spouses, heroes, and everyone who is or was significant in your life.

What do these voices want? They want you to live life their way.

What about your freedom? Well, this book is about exactly that: exercising your freedom.

We will look at how you can willingly listen to the encouraging voices and mute the negative ones.

We want to give you the tools to live a happy, successful and fulfilling life that is aligned with your personal purpose and best self.

Life is a blink. There is no time to waste living under the influence of negative voices. Read this book, share it with others, and learn how to lead a life of freedom and meaning so you can become a beautiful voice in the heads of those around you.

Coming Soon

New Titles

by Michael Kouly

Forget Happiness

THIS IS Leadership